T0159024

J. Edgar Hoover,
Sex, and Crime

J. Edgar Hoover,
Sex, and Crime

J. Edgar Hoover, Sex, and Crime

AN HISTORICAL ANTIDOTE

◻

Athan Theoharis

IVAN R. DEE
Chicago 1995

Library of Congress Cataloging-in-Publication Data:
Theoharis, Athan G.
J. Edgar Hoover, sex, and crime : an historical antidote / Athan
Theoharis.
p.   cm.
Includes bibliographical references and index.
ISBN 1-56663-071-1 (acid-free paper)
1. Hoover, J. Edgar (John Edgar) 1895–1972. 2. United States.
Federal Bureau of Investigation—Officials and employees—Biography.
3. Hoover, J. Edgar (John Edgar) 1895–1972—Sexual behavior.
4. Organized crime—United States—Prevention. I. Title.
HV7911.H6T545   1995
353.0074'092—dc20
[B]   94-36630

CONTENTS

Acknowledgments   7

Introduction   11

ONE. A Compromised Homosexual?

A Case in Search of Evidence   21

TWO. The Politics of Sex   57

THREE. The Politics of Crime   117

CONCLUSION. Hoover, the Law, and Politics   155

A Note on Sources   165

Index   170

ACKNOWLEDGMENTS

RESEARCH for this book was generously funded through grants from the Field Foundation, Warsh-Mott Funds, C. S. Fund, Fund for Investigative Journalism, Webster Woodmansee Fund, Franklin D. Roosevelt Institute, Harry S. Truman Institute, and Marquette University. I have also incurred a large debt to my editor and publisher, Ivan Dee, who not only improved the text through his careful editing but suggested this book in the first place. Responding to my complaints about the shoddy journalism that led to the popularization of Hoover's "homosexuality," he urged me to write this book. I share a larger debt to my wife, Nancy, who has continually supported my research into the history of the FBI and Hoover's directorship while retaining her own skepticism about my seemingly obsessive research interest.

J. Edgar Hoover,
Sex, and Crime

INTRODUCTION

In February 1993 a new biography of the former director of the Federal Bureau of Investigation, J. Edgar Hoover, was published to unusual interest. Written by Anthony Summers—the author of conspiracy-theory books on the Kennedy assassination and on Marilyn Monroe—this best-selling biography quickly and decisively shaped a new public view of Hoover. For its publication coincided with the airing of a Public Broadcasting Corporation "Frontline" documentary on the FBI director (for which Summers had been the principal consultant) and with wire service stories based on a *Vanity Fair* press release highlighting excerpts that the magazine planned to publish from Summers's book. The media's interest centered on Summers's dramatic and salacious revelations that the former FBI director was homosexual, that he had been seen on at least two occasions dressed in drag at homosexual orgies, and that organized-crime bosses, having acquired a compromising photograph of his homosexual activities, had blackmailed Hoover into leaving them alone.

Summers's contentions commanded attention for two reasons. First, for years rumors of Hoover's homosexuality had floated around political Washington and among Hoover's critics nationwide. His lifelong bachelorhood, his preachy denunciations of sexual indiscretions, and his reputation (well founded, as it turns out) for amassing information on the adulterous activities of prominent political leaders had lent credence to these suspicions. In addition, Hoover had a dependent relationship with his mother (whose affection and praise he sought, and with whom he lived until her death in 1938) and a close public relationship with fellow bachelor and FBI Associate Director Clyde Tolson, in whose company he had been regularly seen at lunch, on other social occasions, and on vacation. After Hoover's death in 1972, the bulk of his estate went to Tolson; the two had long been suspected of living together. (Richard Nixon's aide John D. Ehrlichman popularized this last rumor, devoting a long chapter in his memoir on the Nixon White House to a dinner party he had attended with the president at Hoover's residence. There a gaunt Tolson had made a brief appearance in bed clothing. In fact, Hoover and Tolson maintained separate residences, though Tolson at the time was convalescing at Hoover's home following a stay in the hospital for a serious illness.) There was, then, a predisposition to suspect Hoover's homosexuality and to believe the worst—the more so because of revelations dating from the mid-1970s about Hoover's abuses of power as FBI director.

The second reason for the interest aroused by Summers's book was that despite its highly publicized war against "subversives," the FBI under Hoover had done little to help secure indictments of crime bosses. As the story went, Hoover feared that his agents might be corrupted if they tried to infiltrate crime syndicates, and on states' rights grounds he was reluctant to usurp the responsibilities of local and state police forces. For years the FBI director had denied the existence of a Mafia altogether—and then had been caught unawares in November 1957 when a New York state trooper stumbled on a national meeting of Mafia bosses in Apalachin, New York. Embarrassed by this revelation, and still unwilling to concede he had been wrong in denying the Mafia's existence, Hoover belatedly and lamely acknowledged the existence of an organized crime syndicate— but under the name of La Cosa Nostra. This admission, coming at a time when Attorney General Robert Kennedy had appointed a special Justice Department organized-crime strike force, seemed to many critical observers to confirm Hoover's deficiencies as the nation's number one cop.

Summers's book not only tied together these two questions of sex and crime but did so in a particularly captivating way. On two occasions during the 1950s, Summers reported, Hoover had been seen engaging in homosexual activities in a private suite in New York's Plaza Hotel. On the first occasion he was "wearing a fluffy black dress, very fluffy, with flounces and lace stockings and high heels, and a black curly wig." Later that decade he had "a red dress on and a black feather boa around his neck." The image of a homosexual Hoover dressed in drag was so outrageous that it was too good a story to disbelieve. What's more, the "outed" Hoover contrasted starkly with the self-important image cultivated by the publicity-conscious FBI director: a stern puritan, lecturing the public on the immorality of illicit sex and warning of the perils of abandoning traditional family values. With Summers's revelations, Hoover seemed to fall into the company of other recently exposed moralistic charlatans (Jim Bakker and Jimmy Swaggart) who had been caught in the same illicit sexual activities they hypocritically decried. In Hoover's case, his sins were compounded by disclosures that he had maintained secret dossiers on the sexual indiscretions of prominent Americans—including presidents, a First Lady, cabinet officials, and members of Congress.

Summers's allegations almost immediately became a national news story. The Associated Press and Reuters filed summaries of them while the national newspaper *USA Today*, in contrast to the brevity of its coverage of major national and international events, devoted two-thirds of a page to recounting the more lascivious aspects of the "Frontline" exposé. Suspending judgment on the reliability of Summers's documentation, many newspaper editors found this portrayal of Hoover too titillating a story to ignore, in part because of the importance of Hoover's position and the power he had wielded as FBI director for life (his unprecedented forty-eight-year tenure spanned the years from 1924 until his death in 1972). As a result, Summers's portrait quickly became unquestioned Truth—its acceptance promoted by its easy translation into a series of graphic jokes.

Cartoonists and comedians, such as Jay Leno in his introductory monologue to the "Tonight" show, leaped on the revelations about Hoover. When ninety-two-year-old Senator Strom Thurmond first arrived in Washington, Leno quipped, "J. Edgar Hoover was still walking around in a training bra." Hoover had formerly been called "Jedgar Hoover," Leno added, but people now called him "Gay Edgar Hoover." Playing on the 1930s popularization of Hoover's FBI as G-men (government agents), the *New Yorker* depicted Hoover as a "G-man in a G-string" and published two clever cartoons: one showed a doorway bearing the words "The Jaye Edgar Hoover Building" (a play on the name of a homosexual actor in the currently popular British film *The Crying Game*), the second a disconsolate FBI agent rationalizing to another agent, "Has anyone considered that maybe his dress was a disguise?" President Bill Clinton and Republican Senate minority leader Robert Dole entertained a Washington press dinner with similar Hoover jokes. Commenting on the possibility that he might have to replace beleaguered FBI director William Sessions, President Clinton remarked that it would "be hard to fill J. Edgar Hoover's pumps." Senator Dole, in turn, complimented United Press International's Washington bureau chief Helen Thomas on her "lovely dress," adding that it was "from the new J. Edgar Hoover collection."

Although book review editors for the most part failed to take seriously Summers's allegations about Hoover's homosexuality and Mafia blackmailing (a review in the *Washington Post* characterized the book as a "scandalous bestseller" while it merited only a brief dismissive review in the *New York Times Book Review*), cartoonists, comedians, and the writers of President Clinton's and Senator Dole's after-dinner remarks nonetheless were not the principal legitimators of Summers's uncorroborated charges. It was not the *National Enquirer,* the *Star,* "Hard Copy," or "Geraldo" that led the way but the mainstream media—the editors of *Vanity Fair* and *USA Today,* the producers of "Frontline" and the schedulers of the Public Broadcasting Corporation.

Accusations of sexual impropriety have always been part of the treacherous scrutiny of prominent government officials. Moral stature and ethics are undeniably important to assessing fitness for high office, particularly if the official may be in a position to make secret decisions that could compromise the security interests of the nation. But often the intent of circulating scurrilous and uncorroborated charges, from George Washington's through Bill Clinton's presidencies, has been to impugn the character and thereby the programs of prominent national leaders. More often than not, American political campaigns focus on questions of personality (the "character" issue) than on more substantive matters of political philosophy, proposed reforms, and priorities.

Still, the quick acceptance of Summers's account of Hoover's homosexuality, and the media's failure to question his purported evidence, was distinctive. More important, this demeaning portrayal distorts the history of Hoover's directorship of the FBI and the lessons of his lengthy tenure. Summers suggests in effect that character defects and hypocrisy determined both Hoover's abuses of power and the FBI's failure vigorously to pursue organized crime. Had Hoover not been a homosexual, presumably the FBI would not have secretly policed the moral indiscretions of

American political leaders and then pressured them into silent obeisance to the director's political agenda. And, ironically, had Hoover not been so careless in his sexual adventuring, he would not have been vulnerable to blackmail by Mafia bosses—and would not have had to insist that "no single individual or coalition of racketeers dominates organized crime across the Nation."

Summers's account of Hoover's compromised directorship is mind-boggling in its simplicity. How could Hoover alone have successfully stymied the prosecution of organized-crime bosses? To do so would have required the complicity of FBI agents and officials, leading members of Congress, senior officials in the Department of Justice and the White House, and sophisticated Washington-based reporters.

It would not have required great courage for newspaper editors or members of Congress to provide a forum for any FBI agent who might have become frustrated by Hoover's suppression of evidence that might have led to the indictment of organized-crime leaders. Being "soft on crime" and "coddling" Mafia bosses have never been politically tenable positions. The seeming acquiescence of presidents and attorneys general is equally incredible. Since the 1940s presidents have recognized the salience of the crime issue for their political fortunes, especially in appointing their chief campaign adviser to the post of attorney general—J. Howard McGrath (Truman), Herbert Brownell (Eisenhower), Robert Kennedy (Kennedy), John Mitchell (Nixon). From Franklin Roosevelt to Richard Nixon, presidents have pointedly publicized their commitment to protecting the public from criminals. To curb the threat of gangsters and racketeers, President Roosevelt in 1933–1934 lobbied for the enactment of a twelve-point crime program; candidate Nixon, during his run for the presidency in 1968, promised to restore "law and order" while assailing the permissiveness of President Lyndon Johnson's liberal attorney general Ramsey Clark and the anticrime rulings of the Warren Court.

Despite the FBI's poor record against organized crime and Hoover's denials of a nationwide crime conspiracy, the FBI director continued to enjoy popular favor throughout his lengthy tenure and to run the FBI with a heavy hand. Scores of graduates of the nation's law schools eagerly sought an FBI appointment because of the image of the superefficient G-man who successfully apprehended crooks and spies. Why would these hard-line, anticrime agents not defect from the FBI's ranks or, through carefully orchestrated leaks, try to evade the roadblocks imposed by a sexually compromised and hypocritical FBI director? Were ambitious presidents, attorneys general, reporters, and members of Congress blackmailed into silence by an FBI director who had amassed files on their personal and political indiscretions? If so, why has no living attorney general, reporter, or FBI agent, in the wake of Summers's book, surfaced to recite chapter-and-verse examples of stymied investigations and prosecutions?

Hoover's record on organized crime is clearly suspect, whether or not one adopts the G-man standard of always getting your man. And Hoover did have an obsessive interest in monitoring and collecting information about illicit heterosexual affairs, homosexuality, and pornography. But the FBI's collection of such information, and Hoover's file of dossiers on prominent Americans, were due less to defects in his character than to his understanding of the value of such information and how it could serve his political ends if filtered through powerful allies in the White House, the Justice Department, the media, and Congress.

Hoover's power and his virtual untouchability after 1940 derived not from his famed secret files but from his political astuteness. He was, after all, a second-level bureaucrat who ostensibly served at the will of the attorney general. Hoover became powerful and a national icon through the covert relationship he forged with powerful national leaders in the media, the business community, and the federal government—with men who shared his political agenda or who welcomed the many personal favors Hoover's agents performed for them.

Ironically, both Hoover's abuses of power and the FBI's ineffectiveness in pursuing organized-crime leaders stemmed from the same political priorities that ensured him a powerful national following during the cold war years: the belief that he should be accorded broad authority without close oversight in order to help contain the Communist conspiracy. One of the unanticipated costs of this lack of accountability was Hoover's ability to authorize illegal investigative techniques and focus FBI investigations on political activities. As a result, investigating organized crime was not a Hoover priority. And his belated decision to use illegal investigative techniques during criminal investigations actually undermined the FBI's ability to help prosecute (rather than just collect information on) organized-crime leaders.

Hoover's leadership of the FBI can best be understood not in terms of Summers's morality play of compromised homosexuality but as a by-product of the politics and priorities of Cold War America. It is a story of a resourceful bureaucrat who successfully circumvented the limitations of the American constitutional system of checks and balances. In so doing, Hoover compromised the FBI's and the Justice Department's abilities to convict organized-crime leaders. This story of institutional politics remains to be told.

ONE

A Compromised
Homosexual?
A Case
in Search of
Evidence

WAS Hoover a homosexual? Did his sexuality influence his leadership of the FBI and shape the Bureau's investigative priorities? For the Hoover biographer, these are important questions, and not the product of a perverted mind. But the private nature of homosexual conduct makes their resolution extremely difficult, particularly in Hoover's case. Given the moralistic and security-based homophobia of the cold war era, homosexuals were wise to avoid public discovery of their sexual orientation. It was then unquestionably believed that a homosexual would be vulnerable to blackmail and to the betrayal of national secrets. Given the sensitivity of Hoover's position as FBI director, had he been discovered to be homosexual he would have been dismissed or hounded out of government.

Hoover was well aware of this reality from his own experience as FBI director. Twice during President Eisenhower's tenure, for example, he had identified homosexuals on the White House staff, who were then fired. In 1951 he had unilaterally instituted a Sex Deviates program to purge alleged homosexuals from any position in the federal government, from the lowliest clerk to the more powerful position of White House aide. FBI agents were to report even rumored homosexuality—of *anyone*—and to monitor homosexual publications (such as *One*) and homosexual organizations (such as the Mattachine Society and the Daughters of Bilitis). Individuals identified as suspected homosexuals were listed in a Sex Deviates index card file. This information was quietly used to dismiss homosexuals from positions outside the federal government as well, including college professors and police officers.

At the same time Hoover recognized the difficulties of confirming intimations of homosexuality and the counter-productivity of a politics of homosexual rumormongering. His awareness may be seen in three of his actions as FBI director, examples which also indirectly highlight the difficulties confronting any biographer who seeks to understand Hoover's sexuality.

On February 27, 1953, President Dwight Eisenhower nominated Charles Bohlen as United States ambassador to the Soviet Union. Inheriting a vacancy in that position, the recently inaugurated president sought to fill this important post quickly in light of the tensions in U.S-Soviet relations which had been exacerbated by his anti-Communist rhetoric during the presidential campaign. But his proposed nominee caused political problems for the president among the already suspicious McCarthyite wing of the Republican party. Eisenhower had defeated the preferred choice of conservative Republicans, Robert Taft, in gaining the presidential nomination, and did not automatically command the conservatives' loyalty. The McCarthyites' power in

Congress and in state party organizations could complicate Eisenhower's ability to promote his own foreign policy objectives—the dominant issue in national politics, and an issue that separated the president and his moderate Republican supporters from the McCarthyites.

From 1948, and more effectively during the 1952 presidential and congressional campaigns, conservative Republicans had successfully accused the Truman administration of "softness toward communism" and had called for a housecleaning to purge security risks from high government positions, notably the State Department. In these criticisms they had focused on the symbolism of the Yalta Conference of February 1945. At Yalta, the McCarthyites claimed, President Roosevelt and members of the U.S. delegation had sold out Eastern Europe and China, making possible Soviet expansion and laying the basis for the cold war. The Yalta agreements were not simply errors of judgment. Rather, the McCarthyites charged, American security interests and democratic principles had been betrayed by government officials who were either indifferent to or attracted by communism. The McCarthyites welcomed Eisenhower's election for its promise of a militantly anti-Communist foreign policy, with all the "Yalta men" purged from the State Department.

Bohlen's nomination challenged this politics and these expectations. As a career diplomat Bohlen had attended the Yalta Conference as an interpreter for the president and the U.S. delegation. He had publicly defended the Yalta agreements as realistic and in the national interest. For the

McCarthyites, then, Bohlen's nomination raised questions about the future course of Eisenhower's Soviet policy while threatening to undermine a powerful political tool used to discredit liberal Democrats. Because ambassadorial appointments require Senate confirmation, the McCarthyites could either try to defeat this appointment or to use the confirmation process to raise doubts about the president's leadership.

Bohlen's loyalty proved difficult to impugn. His continued defense of Yalta and of other postwar foreign policy positions toward the Soviet Union raised questions about his political judgment but little worse. And the administration argued that Bohlen had been a career diplomat whose role at Yalta had been merely that of an interpreter, and whose appointment to Moscow would be that of a subordinate who represented the administration's foreign policy. The McCarthyites thus looked elsewhere for ammunition to submarine this nomination. One such opportunity involved rumors of Bohlen's homosexuality.

Enjoying direct access to the FBI director, Senator Joseph McCarthy telephoned Hoover on March 18, 1953, to seek his counsel and assistance. Hoover was more than willing to help the senator, in part because he shared the conviction that despite Eisenhower's election "there was practically no change [in State Department loyalty procedures] and everything was running about the same as it was a year ago." The conversation focused on the homosexual question. Responding to McCarthy's inquiry as to "how bad" Bohlen was, Hoover remarked that "this, of course, was very hard to evaluate" because the administration had not requested an FBI investigation "until after Bohlen was named for the appointment." McCarthy pressed Hoover as to whether the FBI director thought Bohlen was a homosexual. Hoover "did not know; that that was a very hard thing to prove and the only way you could prove it was either by admission or by arrest and forfeiture of collateral." This had not occurred "as far as we know" in Bohlen's case, "but it is a fact, and I believe very well known, that he is associating with individuals of that type." Continuing on, Hoover reiterated that "it was very difficult to prove a charge of homosexuality; that he [Bohlen] did associate with such individuals and certainly normally a person did not associate with individuals of that type." Repeating that the FBI "had no evidence to show any overt act" excepting Bohlen's "very bad" judgment in associating with homosexuals, Hoover suggested that the senator could not publicly cite such associations as evidence during the ensuing Senate debate over the Bohlen nomination. McCarthy agreed that "it was so easy to accuse a person of such acts but difficult to prove." Hoover added that such charges were often "used by persons who wanted to smear someone."

McCarthy was clearly disappointed to learn that Hoover could not confirm Bohlen's homosexuality, but he asked if the FBI director could provide him with any information— "public source information such as the Daily Worker"—that he could use during his planned Senate speech denouncing the Bohlen nomination. Hoover lamented that he could not. Even though the FBI had "investigated Bohlen from

27

the security and morals angle," Hoover advised McCarthy, that investigation had been based on interviews with Bohlen's current or past associates in the State Department, and the FBI had not analyzed Bohlen's "political speeches, and so forth, as that was supposedly handled by the State Department."

Much as he might have liked to help McCarthy undercut the president's nominee, Hoover could not provide the needed assistance, and not simply because the FBI had uncovered no evidence to impugn Bohlen's loyalty and character. More important, the FBI's only information had been obtained from interviews with Bohlen's State Department associates and acquaintances, so Hoover could not relay this information to McCarthy without disclosing that McCarthy's source was the FBI. Furthermore, Hoover's suggestion of Bohlen's homosexuality was itself based on unsupported allegations and wild speculation. The FBI's most damning information about Bohlen came from a State Department associate who, during her FBI interview, suggested that Bohlen's "manner of speech indicated effeminacy and she is of definite belief he has strong homosexual tendencies." Although this woman admitted that she had had no social contact with the nominee, she pointed out that Bohlen "walks, acts and talks like a homosexual." She based her assessment on "considerable reading in abnormal psychology in the course of her life, and she has met many homosexuals and claims she is able, with some degree of certainty, to discern homosexual tendencies in individuals." A second FBI source, a State Department security officer, reported that the State Department's index cards on "suspected homosexuals" included one "that Bohlen was associating with sexual perverts." The FBI's third source cited as damning evidence the fact that "an admitted homosexual gave Bohlen as a reference in a Government application."

Interestingly, Hoover did not advise McCarthy that he had already recommended against Bohlen's appointment. On March 17, the day before Hoover's conversation with McCarthy, Secretary of State John Foster Dulles and CIA Director Allen Dulles met with the FBI director to discuss the Bohlen nomination. Advised that the president had requested his personal evaluation, Hoover agreed to abandon his normal practice of not offering any evaluation of the reports compiled by FBI agents during security investigations. "He would not be inclined" to give Bohlen a "complete" security clearance, Hoover responded. He observed that while there "was no direct evidence" of Bohlen's homosexuality, "it was a fact that several of his closest friends and intimate associates were known homosexuals."

In this case Hoover was willing to torpedo Bohlen's nomination on the basis of mere suspicion and speculation, and in the absence of hard evidence. Furthermore, the FBI director, both in his overt contact with the president's representatives and in his covert contact with Senator McCarthy, did so knowing that Eisenhower was committed to the nomination and that the McCarthyites aimed to undermine the president's direction of U.S. foreign policy.

A second, equally revealing example of Hoover's under-

29

standing of the politics of homophobia involved his assistance to another Republican president, Richard Nixon. In this case the FBI director recommended a strategy to prevent the president's adversaries from forcing the dismissal of three high-level White House aides accused of being homosexuals.

The catalyst to this episode was a June 11, 1969, meeting between Jack Anderson, Drew Pearson's collaborator on a syndicated column, and FBI Assistant Director Cartha DeLoach. As head of the FBI's Crime Records Division, DeLoach served as Hoover's liaison to the media and Congress. At this meeting, Anderson advised DeLoach that Pearson had "picked up some very damaging information" that three high-level Nixon aides—H. R. Haldeman, John Ehrlichman, and Dwight Chapin—were homosexuals. Pearson's source, Anderson said, was another White House aide who had provided the columnists with information in the past and was "absolutely reliable." If Pearson were to publish this information in his column it would "be quite a bombshell," Anderson added, but he had advised against publication "until he had further evidence." When DeLoach responded that Anderson's briefing would require the FBI to report this allegation to the White House, Anderson raised no objection but "wanted his name to be kept out of it."

Briefing Hoover on this meeting, DeLoach described Anderson's purpose as "dump[ing]" this information on the FBI "so that he [Pearson] will be in a position to indicate publicly or otherwise, that the FBI had received such information." DeLoach told Hoover that the FBI's investigation of Haldeman, Ehrlichman, and Chapin (pursuant to an earlier presidential security clearance request) had uncovered nothing to indicate the "authenticity" of Pearson's charge. DeLoach then pointed out that Anderson and Pearson had been "very close to [the 1968 Democratic presidential nominee Hubert] Humphrey and he and Pearson have quite naturally been chagrined over the results of the Republican victory."

Hoover immediately briefed President Nixon, Attorney General John Mitchell, and H. R. Haldeman, the president's senior aide. The FBI director then explained how the FBI could help the White House undercut Pearson's and Anderson's hostile intent. He proposed that specially selected FBI officials take "sworn statements" from the three named White House aides denying these allegations; he would then retain these statements in his own office safe. This procedure would preclude any possibility that Pearson could discover and report that the FBI was investigating this allegation, thus denying him the opportunity to make such a claim. Should Pearson claim that the administration had prevented the FBI from investigating the matter, Hoover could produce the signed statements to refute both the charge of a cover-up and the homosexual allegation. In outlining this plan to Haldeman, Hoover began by expressing his own "outrage and disgust" over Anderson's and Pearson's intentions. He advised that it was nonetheless necessary to foreclose the columnists' practice whereby through the circulation of "innuendo they were able to establish [rumor] as fact."

The third case involved Hoover's quiet assistance to President Franklin Roosevelt on the matter of Under Secretary of State Sumner Welles. Returning on the presidential train to Washington, D.C., on September 18, 1940, from the funeral of House Speaker John Bankhead of Alabama, and then on a second train trip later that month from Washington to Cleveland, an inebriated Welles had propositioned a number of porters in his Pullman car. The Secret Service learned in January 1941 that railroad company officials were considering legal action, and brought this to the attention of the president. Roosevelt immediately asked Hoover to conduct a discreet FBI investigation.

Hoover personally briefed the president on the FBI's findings, confirming that the incidents had occurred and, further, that former Ambassador William Bullitt and Senator Burton Wheeler were circulating gossip about Welles. Roosevelt said he suspected that Welles's drinking had precipitated the two incidents, and sought Hoover's counsel. After pointing out that "a great many persons knew of these incidents," Hoover observed that Welles had in fact made these advances—"which was more of a mental condition than anything else and there could not be any assurance it would not be repeated in the future." The FBI director recommended that if the president intended to retain Welles, "certainly someone should be assigned to travel with Mr. Welles to see either that he did not indulge in the use of liquor or that, if he did, that he then did not endeavor to make propositions for such immoral relations." Roosevelt thought this an excellent suggestion.

While the Sumner Welles matter was successfully contained in 1941, it resurfaced as a more troublesome issue in 1942–1943. Secretary of State Cordell Hull, who resented Welles's access to the president, became particularly concerned about rumors of Welles's behavior that were circulating on Capitol Hill. Influential Senate Republicans, notably Ralph Brewster, were demanding information and appropriate action. Roosevelt reluctantly accepted Welles's resignation.

THE Roosevelt, Nixon, and Eisenhower examples illustrate Hoover's interest in homosexual allegations involving high-level public officials, but there was still more. The FBI director's interest virtually exploded whenever such rumors circulated about his own homosexuality. In these instances he would not tolerate a public airing of such allegations but fully employed the resources of the FBI to intimidate his accusers into silence. Identifying the FBI with himself and employing the agency as his personal instrument, Hoover unhesitatingly demanded that FBI agents closely monitor these rumors, alert him to them, and then act forcefully to defend his reputation. The extent and intensity of these efforts made this a high FBI priority.

For example, a 1943 FBI investigation sought to determine whether Washington-based businessman John Monroe had used his "connections in government circles" to secure dismissal of a suit by the wartime Office of Price Administration (OPA) against a Brooklyn baking company. In the course of the inquiry, an FBI agent learned that Monroe had allegedly bragged that he had "no fear of the F.B.I. inasmuch as he 'was the only one who had positive proof that J. Edgar Hoover is a fairy.'" Although this agent reported the allegation to his superior on December 17, 1943, his report was not relayed to Hoover until January 18, 1944. Hoover protested to the head (SAC—special agent in charge) of the FBI's New York field office this "gross" mishandling and demanded to know "why this matter was not reported from Dec 17 to Jan 18." The FBI director did not await the SAC's response. He simultaneously ordered his senior aides to take "vigorous action" to address this failure "to promptly or properly report" the homosexual allegation. Hoover also demanded that Monroe be made to "put up or shut up" concerning his statement.

FBI Assistant Director Louis Nichols was dispatched to confront Monroe and "dress down" and threaten him with "crim[inal] slander unless can prove." During the meeting with Nichols, Monroe denied having made the aspersion, claiming to have been himself the victim of character assassination.* He signed a statement to that effect. Hoover did not believe this denial, and Monroe remained a subject of FBI investigative interest. Although he escaped indictment in the 1943 case, Monroe was indicted in 1945 and convicted in 1946 for violating OPA price ceilings.

*Monroe was at the time involved in a libel suit with syndicated columnist Drew Pearson, and advised Nichols of his suspicion that Pearson had passed this rumor to the FBI.

Letters of reprimand were placed in the personnel files of the New York FBI officials who had supervisory responsibility over this 1943 investigation and who had failed to report and act immediately upon this homosexual allegation. These officials were further admonished that "No repetition will be tolerated." Finally, E. E. Conroy, the New York SAC, convened two meetings of all the supervisors in the New York office at which he conveyed his "very forceful" displeasure over their failure to have "immediately called" such "scandalous and scurrilous remarks" about Hoover to his immediate attention.

New York agents, and those assigned to other field offices, learned an important lesson: their careers and future advancement in the FBI would be determined by how closely they monitored and immediately reported any derogatory comments about Hoover's character—no matter how innocuous or incredible. In due course, ever-alert agents reported to the FBI director a variety of gossipy allegations, whether by a woman at a meeting of her bridge club in Cleveland, a beauty parlor operator to a customer in Washington, D.C., or a Detroit businessman to his host during a visit to New York City. Each offender was thereupon visited by a high-level FBI official and subjected to intimidating interviews.

The woman who had remarked at the Cleveland bridge party that she had heard that Hoover was homosexual was so chastised by the Cleveland SAC that she agreed at the next meeting of her bridge club "to point out to each of those present that her statement was not founded on fact and that she was deeply sorry that she had made it and it should not have been made at all." The Washington, D.C., beauty parlor operator was interviewed twice by two senior FBI officials (an FBI assistant director and an FBI supervisor) at her place of business. She denied having made scurrilous remarks about Hoover, including a suggestion that he was "queer," and was "advised in no uncertain terms that such statements . . . would not be countenanced." Reporting back to Hoover, FBI Assistant Director F. C. Holloman contended that this woman "fully realizes the seriousness of her accusations, and it is not believed that she will ever be guilty of such statements."

In a report on his interview with the Detroit businessman, the Detroit SAC described him as "scared to death" that the FBI was "going to investigate him." The interviewing agent had warned the businessman that if he ever again called Hoover a homosexual he "might take care of him right there on the spot." The Detroit SAC confidently predicted that this man "will not repeat such a statement in the future." The mind-set of FBI personnel was best expressed by Louisville SAC M. W. McFarlin: Hoover could be assured that "so long as there is a Federal Bureau of Investigation that those associated with you will exert every means in their power to protect you from malicious lying attacks and throw the lies down the throats of those who utter them."

If Hoover had his agents move quickly to intimidate those who questioned his sexuality during essentially private conversations, he upped the ante whenever such allegations might be widely disseminated. Having heard that *Los Angeles Times* reporter Jack Nelson planned to write a critical article on himself and the FBI, including reports that the director was homosexual, Hoover arranged a meeting with Nelson's bosses at which he sought to have Nelson fired. Hoover cited instances of Nelson's excessive drinking (the FBI's only derogatory information on this reporter) and claimed to have learned that Nelson had been given the "assignment of 'getting' me, and . . . was assigned to the Washington bureau of the Los Angeles *Times* for this specific purpose." Hoover's threats proved unavailing; instead Nelson's standing with his superiors improved. For this sin the *Times* was placed on Hoover's "not to contact" list and was denied help on pending stories.

Hoover was more successful in a second case. *New York Times* reporter Anthony Leviero, Hoover learned, had been commissioned by *American Mercury* publisher Lawrence Spivak to write "a highly critical 'smear' article in the nature of a profile" which would charge Hoover "with perversion," contend that Hoover claimed "personal credit" for the accomplishments of local police, other government departments, and the FBI, and that "while constantly disclaiming that there is any political consideration in your [Hoover's] policies, you are, nevertheless, a most successful politician."

To contain this threat, Hoover mounted an attack on several fronts. FBI Associate Director Clyde Tolson belligerently accosted Spivak in a restaurant to inquire how his "smear article" was coming along while FBI Assistant

Director Louis Nichols quietly interceded with *Reader's Digest* general editor Paul Palmer, a former partner of Spivak's on the *American Mercury*, to kill the critical article. Nichols also met with both Leviero and Spivak. In his meeting with Nichols, Leviero denied any intention to write a "smear" piece. Spivak, a political conservative and a journalist of considerable stature, said he had originally sought a meeting with Hoover to dispel any doubts about the nature of the article. Affirming his interest in publishing an "objective piece and nothing else," Spivak assured Nichols that he intended to "check each fact and triple check it and if there was anything that was the least bit derogatory he would check it with Mr. Hoover personally." At the end of this meeting, Nichols promised to brief Hoover on Spivak's assurances, and singled out the "element of perversion" as having most "infuriated" Hoover, Tolson, and himself. When Nichols reported back to Spivak that the FBI director had accepted his apology and considered the "incident closed," Spivak, in a revealing comment, characterized this as "a wonderful demonstration of a free country, that had this occurred in any other country he would have been shot by now." Not surprisingly, perhaps, Leviero decided against writing the profile.

Clearly, one did not lightly remark about Hoover's sexuality. The intensity of his interest and his commitment to stifle such rumors demonstrated, at a minimum, Hoover's awareness of their damage not only to his personal reputation but to his tenure as FBI director. Hoover's concern to retain his office obliged him to conduct his personal life in a way that precluded the possibility of anyone discovering whether he was a practicing homosexual. As a cautious, highly disciplined bureaucrat who had devised special records procedures to conceal his authorization of "clearly illegal" activities or his receipt of highly confidential reports, Hoover would never have put himself in a position where anyone, other than a homosexual lover, could uncover such a dangerous secret.

This reality renders incredible Anthony Summers's most electrifying source—Susan Rosenstiel, who claimed to have seen Hoover, in 1958 and then again in 1959, dressed in drag and engaged in homosexual orgies hosted by former McCarthy aide Roy Cohn at the Plaza Hotel in New York. The former Mrs. Rosenstiel would have us believe that Hoover allowed himself, not once but twice within a year, to be observed while participating in homosexual activities. It is impossible to confirm or refute such activity during the 1950s in a private suite in the Plaza Hotel—had such parties taken place, only those present could contradict Susan Rosenstiel, and all those she names are deceased. The private nature of such activity ensured that its existence could have become known only if someone in attendance decided to come forward.

Could Hoover have been surprised in the act, as Mrs. Rosenstiel claims? In attending these orgies and dressing in drag, had he anticipated that no one, except those who were homosexuals like himself and who shared his interest in not being caught, would see him in such a compromising position? Why, moreover, would Susan Rosenstiel have attended a homosexual orgy? Her explanation renders an incredible account even more incredible.

Susan Rosenstiel was at the time of the alleged parties the fourth wife of Lewis Rosenstiel, the multimillionaire owner of Schenley Industries. Rosenstiel had made his fortune in the liquor industry in the years after Prohibition, allegedly through his contacts with organized crime. Ultra-conservative in politics and sensitive to his own public relations problems, Rosenstiel in 1957 lured Louis Nichols into early retirement* to become a Schenley vice president at a reported annual salary of $100,000. Nichols, seeking to refurbish Rosenstiel's image, convinced the multimillionaire in 1965 to make an initial gift of $1 million to endow the J. Edgar Hoover Foundation at Valley Forge, Pennsylvania. The stated mission of this foundation was "to safeguard the heritage of freedom of the United States of America and to perpetuate the ideas to which the Honorable J. Edgar Hoover has dedicated his life ... [and] to combat Communism." The foundation sought to inculcate American youth with the importance of "Americanism" by funding educational programs, scholarships, and endowed chairs as well as magazines, books, and pamphlets.

While he was never a close friend of Hoover, Rosenstiel's hiring of Nichols earned him ready access to the vain FBI director, who throughout his tenure had regularly sought to curry favor with prominent businessmen. According to Susan Rosenstiel, however, her second husband and Roy

---

*At the time Nichols was the number three man in the FBI hierarchy behind Hoover and Tolson, and Hoover's public relations genius.

Cohn in 1958 invited her to attend a party in Cohn's hotel suite at the Plaza on the condition of secrecy, with Cohn adding, "You're in for a big surprise." She explains that Lewis Rosenstiel extended this invitation because her first husband, to whom she had been married for nine years, had been "predominantly" homosexual. So Lewis Rosenstiel had concluded that she "was a 'regular' and knew what life was, that my first husband had been gay and I must have understood because I'd stayed with him for nine years." At the 1958 party, and on a second occasion in 1959 (for which she stated that she was paid off with an expensive pair of earrings), she witnessed Hoover engage in homosexual activities, dressed in drag.

The story is unbelievable and reflects more about Susan Rosenstiel's attitudes toward men in general.* Claiming that both her first and second husbands were homosexual (her second husband bisexual), and that her discovery of her first husband's homosexuality led to their divorce after nine years of marriage, she would have us believe that she twice attended homosexual orgies—the first time on a dare and the second because of a bribe of expensive earrings. Her malicious portrait of Lewis Rosenstiel (she further claims that at the first party he "wanted me to get involved [with two boys] but I wouldn't do it") leaves unexplained why he

*In addition to linking Hoover with Cohn, another rumored homosexual, Susan Rosenstiel claims that Cohn flaunted his homosexuality to her and told her about her husband's other homosexual friends, notably Cardinal Spellman (another rumored homosexual). She thereby links together a veritable Who's Who of rumored homosexuals (Hoover, Cohn, Spellman), with her first and second husbands thrown in for free.

would want her present at two homosexual parties which could only adversely affect their relationship. Nor can she explain why she had not sought a divorce from Rosenstiel after the "surprise" of the first party, given her further claim to having earlier caught him "in bed" with Roy Cohn, and why she had not raised the matter of homosexuality in her own later pleas for divorce.

But Susan Rosenstiel's story gets better. In addition to seeing Hoover wearing a dress, hose, heels, and a wig, she claims to have watched him engage in homosexual activities at the first party with two eighteen- to nineteen-year-old blond males, and at the second party with two boys dressed in leather. On this second occasion, she reports, "Hoover had a Bible. He wanted one of the boys to read from the Bible. And he read, I forget which passage, and the other boy played with him [Hoover], wearing the rubber gloves. And then Hoover grabbed the Bible, threw it down and told the second boy to join in the sex."

Nothing is missing: a homosexual Hoover in drag, engaging in sex with blond boys dressed in leather and—continuing this stereotypically homophobic account—with a Bible being held, read from, and then discarded. No fundamentalist minister could better capture the immorality of homosexuals!

Susan Rosenstiel, moreover, was not a disinterested party. Although the target of her allegations was J. Edgar Hoover, she managed as well to defame her second husband with whom she had been involved in a bitterly contested divorce which lasted ten years in the courts. Her hatred of Lewis

Rosenstiel had led her in 1970 to offer damaging testimony about his alleged connections with organized-crime leaders before a New York state legislative committee on crime. This testimony remains sealed and cannot be evaluated for its credibility.

Susan Rosenstiel was not Summers's sole incredible source. He provided further corroboration of Hoover's homosexuality by reporting that Hoover's concerns about it had led him to seek the counsel of a Washington, D.C., psychiatrist, Dr. Marshall deG. Ruffin.* On its face, this account is more believable. If Hoover was homosexual, he could have been so troubled by his sexual orientation, his own hypocrisy in publicly denouncing "perverted" sex, and his own aggressive efforts to purge homosexuals from government that he sought psychiatric counsel. The contradiction between his private life and public activities would have been wrenching, and he might have felt anxious that his continued indulgence might result in his being caught, with resulting public humiliation. Visiting a psychiatrist offered the prospect of medical assistance and an assurance of secrecy; psychiatrists are professionally bound to honor the confidentiality of a doctor-patient relationship.

---

*Summers's source, apparently, was either syndicated columnist Jack Anderson or a February 1971 Anderson column in which he claimed that Hoover had "consulted" a psychiatrist, naming Dr. Ruffin. Incensed by this published defamation, Hoover that same month inquired of Deputy Attorney General Richard Kleindienst whether he should sue Anderson. Kleindienst's sarcastic response reflected his low estimate of the reliability of Anderson's column—that "if Anderson had spelled my [Hoover's] name right, to leave it alone."

In light of Hoover's powerful position and the recent disclosures of his abuses of power (including monitoring the sexual activities of prominent political leaders), a psychiatrist with political principles might well have concluded that it was more ethical to expose Hoover to reporters or authors. Presumably Ruffin could have documented his professional relationship with Hoover through appointment records, and through case notes have recorded Hoover's admissions.

Summers's source, however, was not Dr. Ruffin, who died in 1984, but his widow. Recounting her husband's counseling sessions with Hoover, she added that he had "burned" his notes shortly before his death. As in the case of Susan Rosenstiel, we are left with an uncorroborated account, in this case of a widow who, during a 1990 interview, precisely dates her husband's counseling sessions with Hoover as occurring "in late 1946" and then "again later in 1971."

There is further reason to question this account. When I began researching my own biography of Hoover during the 1980s, I became the recipient of numerous volunteered examples of Hoover's homosexuality (although none as melodramatic as that of Susan Rosenstiel). Each of the allegations turned out to be baseless, either because records that would have confirmed the allegations had been destroyed or because what was being offered was an eyewitness account. A principal source of these rumors was the gay community—which had its own interest in "outing" Hoover, whether to expose his hypocritical homophobia or to show that homosexuals could hold sensitive government positions without compromising national security. Among the proffered examples was the psychiatrist story—which Summers attributed to Dr. Ruffin. I was not told the name of the psychiatrist, or that he was already deceased. If I was interested in pursuing this matter, I was told, contact would be made with the psychiatrist's son to see whether he would be willing to disclose his and his father's identity. I demurred, having decided first to determine the credibility of Hoover's psychiatric counseling by contacting the person identified as having referred Hoover to the psychiatrist. Summers reports that Hoover's personal physician, Dr. William Clark, had referred him to Dr. Ruffin; but I had been told that former Senator J. William Fulbright had provided this referral.

It struck me as incredible that Hoover would approach Fulbright (a brilliant lawyer and astute when it came to foreign affairs, but with no special expertise in the area of psychiatric referral) and disclose his interest in seeing a psychiatrist. Such an interest might not betray his homosexuality, but it certainly would have alerted a prominent senator, who was not friendly to Hoover, to the FBI director's need for psychiatric counseling. True, Hoover could have avoided this political problem and obtained better counsel from Dr. Clark, his personal physician, but even that request carried the risk of disclosing Hoover's troubled mental state. Absolute confidentiality was possible: Hoover might have instead relied upon the FBI's resources to obtain the names of reputable psychiatrists in the Washington, D.C., area, ostensibly to seek consultation on the workings of the criminal mind. In any event, I did contact Fulbright, who (perhaps more gently than my request deserved) denied that he had made such a referral.

Summers's third sources—and from these he segues into Hoover's blackmailing by organized-crime leaders—claim to have seen a photograph of Hoover and Tolson engaging in a homosexual act. None of those who told Summers they had seen this photograph produced a copy; they simply testified to having seen it. According to Summers, John Weitz, a former official in the wartime Office of Strategic Services (OSS), had been shown the photograph in the early 1950s at a dinner party hosted by the former head of the CIA's counterintelligence division, James Angleton. Summers also recounts a second viewing by a self-proclaimed intelligence operative, Gordon Novel. According to Novel, in 1967, with the support of the Johnson White House and the CIA, he was pursuing a lawsuit against New Orleans prosecutor Jim Garrison. Hoover opposed his investigation, Novel said, and he was advised that he would incur Hoover's wrath if he continued it. Novel sought a meeting with James Angleton, who urged him to continue and then took from his desk the compromising photograph of Hoover and Tolson and told him "to go see Hoover and tell him I'd seen the sex photographs." According to Novel, this photograph, a copy of which found its way into the hands of organized-crime leaders, had been taken by the OSS in 1946 at a time when that agency "was fighting [the FBI] over foreign intelligence which Hoover wanted but never got." Novel recounted that he then met Hoover at the Mayflower Hotel in Washington. Upon being advised that Novel had been sent by Angleton and had "seen the sex photographs," an infuriated Hoover eventually relented and Novel proceeded, no longer impeded by the FBI director.

The implication of this tale is that Hoover became a victim of a struggle between the FBI and the OSS for control of foreign intelligence. But the story is both unbelievable and fictitious. OSS agents could not have taken this compromising photograph in 1946, for the agency was dissolved by President Truman in September 1945, its personnel either retired or assigned to other agencies. In 1946 Truman created a Central Intelligence Group (the immediate predecessor to the CIA), but its personnel were on temporary assignment from the established intelligence agencies—State, FBI, MID (Military Intelligence Division), and ONI (Office of Naval Intelligence). Nor was the FBI the OSS's principal bureaucratic rival. Before World War II only State, ONI, and MID conducted foreign intelligence, and their officials were more intensely concerned than the FBI about the creation of a rival agency having direct access to the president. OSS director William Donovan and Hoover were indeed rivals (and Hoover's FBI closely monitored Donovan's personal and official activities), but Donovan would not have risked the discovery of his agents' participation in a break-in to install photographic equipment in Hoover's residence. Had he done so, Donovan would have used this compromising photograph to force Hoover's dismissal—less for bureaucratic than for security reasons, given the prevailing notion that a homosexual could be blackmailed into betraying security information.

It is inconceivable that someone of Novel's background could have obtained an interview with Angleton. And in light of Angleton's recognized obsession with security, it is unimaginable that the CIA chief would have shared such a compromising photograph with Novel. Had he possessed such a photograph, Angleton would have already shown it to the CIA director, the attorney general, and the president— again, for security reasons. This delightful story also leaves unexplained why Angleton did not use the photograph to advance the CIA's interests. Such a photograph would have come in handy in 1970, at a time when Hoover had severed the FBI's liaison relationship with the CIA and had cut back the FBI's various intelligence services to the CIA (foreign embassy break-ins and electronic surveillance).

What really happened was this. In June 1944 an OSS official named Towell contacted the head of the FBI's wartime security division to obtain permission for an OSS agent to "select copies of obscene material" from FBI files. The material was to be used to counteract a Japanese program of "sending obscene photographs of American girls through India and other countries in an effort to create the impression of lax morals on the part of Americans." The OSS planned to disseminate "similar material with reference to Japanese girls through this same area." When he was advised that the FBI had "a collection of 25 to 30 photographs of this nature" in its Obscene File, Hoover allowed an OSS agent to "obtain copies of a representative group of these photographs for this project."

OSS and then CIA officials were thereafter aware of this FBI capability. In May 1951 Joseph Bryan III,* then employed in the CIA's psychological warfare division, received CIA and FBI authorization to review the FBI's Obscene File. It remains unclear why CIA officials sought such assistance in 1951, and what uses were then made of the contents of the FBI's Obscene File. In any event, on the eve of the 1952 presidential election, Bryan hosted a dinner party in his home. After remarking to his guests about Hoover's perverse interest in pornography, Bryan reportedly then stated that the FBI director "had a crush on a friend of theirs and had made advances to him several times; when it was found out that no progress could be made, [Hoover] had 'turned him in.' " Bryan claimed to be able to identify this person and "would be glad to testify to it and he could name this person and prove it," adding that Hoover was "afraid of me for this reason."

Inevitably, Hoover was informed of Bryan's alleged statements. Incensed by Bryan's disclosure of the contents of the Obscene File, Hoover demanded a briefing. The FBI director was reminded that he had earlier authorized Bryan and a second CIA officer to review the Obscene File, but on the condition that "someone from the Security Division should

*A member of a prominent Virginia family—his father was the publisher of the *Richmond News Leader*—Bryan had joined the CIA in 1947. He left the agency in 1952 to become special assistant to the secretary of the air force.

accompany them." Hoover then ordered that henceforth this file "should not be exhibited to anyone outside [the FBI] unless specifically authorized by Tolson or myself."

Hoover also demanded that FBI officials contact the source of the report on this dinner party, learn the names of all those in attendance, and seek confirmation of what had been said. Hoover insisted that Bryan "be made to put up or shut up. I want no effort to be spared to call his bluff and promptly." To ensure that all identified parties were fully responsive, Hoover directed his aides to impress upon the CIA liaison that the FBI director expected full cooperation. If the CIA and the other identified parties failed to cooperate, Hoover intended to "arrange for a congressional committee to subpoena [Bryan] or will file suit for slander or initiate Criminal Slander proceedings in D.C. Court."

The resulting FBI interviews proved unavailing. Although the FBI's source repeated his account of this dinner party, he demurred about going public, expressing concern about Bryan's influence and slippery character. Others identified as having attended the party denied having heard Bryan make the alleged statement. Unable to resolve conflicting versions, Hoover and his close aides decided not to press for a congressional investigation or even to interview Bryan.

The Bryan matter did not die, however. In 1955 Hoover learned from the FBI's "friendly sources on the Hill" that Bryan had repeated the allegation about Hoover's homosexuality to another individual who in turn had reported it during a meeting in the office of the vice chairman of the Senate Internal Security Subcommittee, William Jenner.

Having concluded that the FBI now had "enough evidence in this matter to tackle Joseph Bryan and make him put up or shut up," FBI Assistant Director Louis Nichols requested Hoover's approval for himself and FBI supervisor Cartha DeLoach to interview Bryan. Nichols assured Hoover that "no holds will be barred," that he personally wanted the pleasure of making Bryan "put up or shut up." The FBI assistant director also emphasized that the FBI "should really try to make an issue" in view of Bryan's former CIA employment—he knew "better than to be permitted to get by with such."

Hoover approved this request, and Nichols and DeLoach interviewed Bryan at his home. Told that the FBI had learned of his alleged remarks about Hoover's homosexuality at the 1952 dinner party, Bryan claimed that his comments had been misreported. During a discussion with one of his guests about "rumors and gossip in Washington," he said, he had innocently remarked that he "wouldn't be surprised to hear that Admiral [William] Halsey* was beating his wife or that J. Edgar Hoover was a homosexual." Nichols countered that the FBI had learned that Bryan had repeated the statement to another person that month—and the FBI had a signed statement from this individual. A distraught Bryan repeated his denial and wrote Hoover: "I can only give you my word that never did I utter any such statement.

*Bryan had published a biography of Halsey in 1947. Coincidentally, that same year he had sought and obtained an interview with Hoover for a planned profile of the FBI director for the *Saturday Evening Post*. Bryan never published this profile, having in the interim joined the CIA.

I do not slander anyone. Specifically, I do not tell lies. I hope most sincerely that you will believe this."

Hoover and Nichols did not believe Bryan's denial.* Nichols had pointedly warned Bryan that the FBI did not intend to "permit such statements to go unchallenged," and that should such allegations ever be repeated, "anyone who said it would have to put up or shut up and we would take care of anyone who made such a statement." Nor was this an idle threat. Nichols thereupon briefed Senate Internal Security Subcommittee counsel Jay Sourwine about the FBI's "experience with Bryan and his denial," on the understanding that Sourwine would brief Senator Jenner. The FBI's liaison to the CIA, Sam Papich, also briefed his CIA contact about this 1955 incident and the FBI's possession of the signed statement from Bryan's accuser. If the intent was to smear Bryan to his former CIA employers, a further purpose was to raise questions about the professionalism and discretion of CIA personnel.

In any event, John Weitz's version bears little relationship to the quite different and more complex reality. CIA and OSS officials had never been in the business of monitoring Hoover's personal conduct. Instead they had sought to promote closer cooperation with the vain and difficult FBI director. Given their interest in preserving the confidentiality of classified records and in ensuring an effective internal security program, these officials would never have allowed

---

*Bryan repeated it in 1981 when I interviewed him. It was some thirty years later, and Hoover was dead, but Bryan was still defensive and quite nervous.

organized-crime leaders to obtain information that might compromise the FBI's law enforcement efforts.

What other evidence, then, did Summers offer about the Mafia's blackmailing of Hoover? Summers recounted the claims of a number of organized-crime figures (Seymour Pollack, Jimmy Fratianno, Irving Resnick) that they learned of Hoover's homosexuality and cited instances wherein this information had been used to pressure the FBI director not to prosecute crime leaders. The criminal backgrounds of these men raises serious questions about the veracity of their accusations—and they bore no love for Hoover or interest in upholding his reputation. Ironically, in offering an insider's account of a conspiracy to protect criminals, Summers relies on the very technique that Hoover himself successfully employed during the cold war years to further the anti-Communist "cause" (FBI Assistant Director Louis Nichols's revealing phrasing).

When they promoted the second Red Scare as part of a formal "educational campaign" initiated in February 1946, FBI officials relied directly and indirectly on the testimony of ex-Communists. During Smith Act trials or as friendly witnesses before congressional committees such as the House Committee on Un-American Activities or the Senate Internal Security Subcommittee, these former Communists publicly described the true purposes of the Communist conspiracy. FBI officials, with Hoover's approval, had provided the congressional committees with the names of many of these ex-Communists, having recognized the value of congressional hearings in providing a public forum to expose the sinister nature of the Communist conspiracy.

Many of these ex-Communists—notably Louis Budenz—embellished their testimony, offering new names of party members as the occasion warranted, or tortured exegeses as to which Communist statements were to be believed as literal truth and which were "Aesopian" language intended to mislead. Hoover's rationale for believing them was that as former participants in the Communist conspiracy they were in a privileged position to know and reveal the truth. The secretive nature of the Communist conspiracy dictated that the truth could be learned only when former conspirators decided to inform—and in such cases one could not expect other documentary corroboration. Hoover's commitment to promoting the truthfulness of ex-Communist informers also underlay his aggressive response in the case of Harvey Matusow, an informer who in 1955 recanted his earlier testimony and claimed that he had been pressured by FBI and Justice Department officials to give perjurious testimony. Hoover denounced the repentant Matusow as unreliable and charged that his recantation was itself part of the Communist conspiracy to discredit principled informers. In 1960 Hoover also rallied to the defense of the House Committee on Un-American Activities, then under attack because of its reliance on the unconfirmed allegations of ex-Communists who publicly exposed Communists and Communist sympathizers during highly publicized hearings. Decrying the efforts of those who sought to abolish the committee, Hoover praised the committee's method of exposure, for the nation's security could be preserved only through publicizing the testimony of ex-Communists.

Summers turned the table on Hoover. Whether in the cases of Susan Rosenstiel or Seymour Pollack, he presented uncorroborated allegations of claimed coconspirators as undeniable truth—for only those attending private sex orgies or privy to the secret discussions of organized-crime leaders could have provided evidence of Hoover's homosexuality and blackmailing by the Mob. It might be satisfying to conclude that Hoover richly deserves Anthony Summers as his biographer. But Summers's sources, if undeniably imaginative, provide no credible documentation for what amounts to no more than gossipy character assassination.

Whether or not Hoover was homosexual—and I doubt that he was—the wily and cautious FBI director would never have put himself in a position that publicly compromised his sexuality. His personal obsession was to retain the FBI directorship. His abilities were those not of a sophisticated criminologist but of a politically astute bureaucrat with a brilliant strategic mind who traded in information and operated in secret. Willing to abuse his office to advance his own political and moralistic agenda, Hoover's strategic vision led him to devise procedures to ensure that his most serious abuses could not be uncovered. If he was a practicing homosexual, he would also have taken whatever safeguards were needed to ensure that such a dark secret would go with him to his grave.

TWO

The Politics
of Sex

O N May 10, 1924, Attorney General Harlan Fiske Stone appointed J. Edgar Hoover acting director of the Bureau of Investigation (it was not formally renamed the Federal Bureau of Investigation until 1935). Hoover had been an assistant director of the Bureau, and his promotion was probationary. Stone did not make the appointment permanent until December of that year. A series of revelations that Bureau agents had monitored the activities of congressional critics of the Harding administration and had investigated labor union and political activists during the years 1920 to 1924 led Stone to fire the current director, William Burns, and to institute strict rules to prevent the recurrence of these abuses. The Bureau was barred from wiretapping and from investigating "political or other opinions of individuals...[except for] such conduct as is forbidden by the laws of the United States."

Stone's restrictions were intended to stanch a scandal that might damage the political fortunes of the Calvin Coolidge administration. The attorney general's companion warning—that a "police system" which exceeded its law enforcement responsibilities could endanger the "proper administration of justice and...human liberty"—also captured the prevailing ethos of the United States in the mid-1920s. With their strong states' rights and laissez-faire convictions, America's political and business leaders endorsed a government of narrowly defined powers, fearing that federal officials would otherwise intrude on state responsibilities, privacy rights, and economic liberties. These fears had seemingly been confirmed by the Bureau's intrusive and politically motivated investigations under Burns, and the publicized abuses had raised the question of the value of the Bureau itself. Did its potential benefit to federal law enforcement outweigh its dangers to constitutional rights?

As the newly appointed director, Hoover recognized the perils of his situation. He would have to refurbish the Bureau's image and establish its usefulness while respecting popular fears of a too powerful centralized government. He set out to convey the sense that the Bureau's past abuses had been a result of the personnel practices of his predecessors, announcing that appointments were now to be based on merit not patronage, and that only highly trained professionals were to be recruited as agents—graduates of law schools and accountants (the latter because the Bureau's investigations of interstate commerce and antitrust violations required economic expertise). To publicize the Bureau's usefulness, Hoover announced the establishment of a nationwide fingerprinting center. The mobility of the population had made it difficult for local police forces to monitor criminals. Local crime-fighting capabilities would benefit from a centralized fingerprint depository with the Bureau's role being merely that of a servicing agency. Finally, although Hoover did not comply with Stone's ban on political surveillance—devising reporting procedures that would minimize the discovery of the Bureau's continued monitoring of radical activities—he sent Stone a copy of his directive to the heads of the Bureau's field offices: "the activities of the Bureau are to be limited strictly to investigations of violations of the federal statutes."

This low-profile strategy did not mean that Hoover was resigned to a functionary role, passively awaiting public approval. He recognized the Bureau's limited law enforcement responsibilities (only with the New Deal of the 1930s did federal authority explode) but astutely exploited another dimension of the politics of the day—a moralistic concern about personal conduct. Prohibition reflected this concern, as did the conviction that sexual licentiousness undermined traditional Christian values. Moral righteousness underlay the widespread appeal of religious fundamentalist preachers like Billy Sunday and Aimee Semple during the 1920s and even the acceptance of the Ku Klux Klan, one of whose planks called for a campaign against adultery. A politics of sex thus very early became part of Hoover's public relations strategy to establish the quality of his leadership, restore the Bureau's reputation, develop a popular constituency, and undercut states' rights opposition to an expanded role for federal law enforcement.

Stone's 1924 orders had limited the Bureau's investigative responsibilities to enforcing federal laws. At the time this meant investigating violations of interstate commerce

and antitrust laws, including such essentially immoral activities as the distribution and sale of obscene literature
and the recruitment of women for prostitution.

Hoover not only moved quickly to enforce these popular
laws but did so with maximum publicity. As early as March
24, 1925, the new director created a new centralized
depository for "obscene and improper" materials acquired
by Bureau agents. Agents were ordered to forward to Bureau
headquarters in Washington "all obscene matter such as
booklets, leaflets, photographic prints, etc." in a "sealed"
envelope or package marked in capital letters "OBSCENE."
These submissions were then to be filed separate from
other Bureau reports. The creation of this centralized
depository in the FBI Laboratory helped to preclude discovery
that the FBI maintained such material to promote prosecution and for publicity value.

Heads of field offices (SACs) were specifically admonished
to submit "immediately" all "obscene exhibits...at the
earliest possible moment...[and] prior to presenting the
facts and exhibits to the appropriate U.S. Attorney for a
prosecutive opinion." Whether or not prosecution was
recommended, obscene exhibits were to be reviewed, com-
pared with other such exhibits, and "included as a permanent part of the Obscene File or destroyed when no
purpose could be served by [permanently] filing the exhibit."
The FBI's permanent collection included "true pornography,"
such as stag movies, photographs, books, pamphlets, free-
hand drawings, comic strip cartoons, and playing cards.
By July 1966 this permanent collection had grown to 1,364

"obscene and nude art motion picture films," 321 phonograph records, 3,020 readers and pamphlets, 895 "obscene books, nudist publications and questionable periodicals," 5,611 cartoon booklets, 183 playing cards, 1,593 cards containing "obscene and strip type photographs," and 163 pieces of "advertising literature (by companies involved)." This mass had been built up over the years with, for example, the FBI Laboratory receiving 10,458 "obscene" specimens during the year 1965–1966, which were then considered for inclusion in the permanent Obscene File.

The collection of such materials might pose public relations problems if FBI officials were to seek prosecution for materials they wrongfully deemed obscene. To preclude the embarrassing disclosure that agents were collecting materials protected under the First Amendment,* Hoover insisted that SACs "closely" monitor "all obscene matter" investigations to avoid any criticism that FBI investigations "involve such items as pin-up pictures, art poses, nudist photographs or magazines, parlor novelties, or other exhibits obviously not obscene or which are of highly questionable obscenity." Such materials were nonetheless to be collected and forwarded because they might be useful for future prosecution. Hoover's rationale reflected his own puritanical

*In one case in the 1940s (the so-called Varga Girl case), the courts had overturned the Post Office Department's revocation of the second-class mailing privileges of *Esquire* magazine because of its drawings of girls in sexy poses.

and authoritarian values.* Commenting on the "general practice" of commercial "purveyors of obscene materials... to disseminate their products among school children and adults with perverted minds," Hoover required that all acquired "obscene materials" be forwarded to the FBI Laboratory "regardless of the source from which they are obtained. Even though no Federal violation exists, any material of this nature made available by local police agencies should be transmitted to the Bureau in order to increase the effectiveness of the Obscene File."

In certain circumstances Hoover also endorsed prosecution of obscene cases to force the courts to reverse their rulings based on the First Amendment. In a 1970 conversation with President Richard Nixon, he urged that the Justice Department challenge recent Supreme Court rulings written by Justices Hugo Black and William Douglas and pursue cases developed from the seizure of foreign obscene literature in New York and Washington, D.C. By pressing these cases and publicizing the contents of the seized material, Hoover counseled, the administration could force the Court to reassess its refusal to "declare obscene that which is raw obscenity." Vigorous prosecution would allow the Justice Department "to get some publicity out that the country is sick of this crap they see in the newsstands."

Hoover astutely recognized how obscene investigations

---

*Hoover also sought to limit access by FBI agents to the Obscene File, warning that when obscene material was "in the office, it must not be shown to other personnel in the office who have no need to observe it.... There should be no undue curiosity about such filth."

could further the FBI's stature. "Each obscene investigation," he advised SACs, "possesses potential publicity value" and thus should be "closely" followed to obtain "proper publicity." Whenever "publicity will result from the Bureau's investigation of an obscene matters case," SACs were to notify FBI headquarters "in advance of any contemplated arrest, arraignment, or other development prior to the time that any publicity is released."

Obscenity cases helped promote Hoover's bureaucratic interests and undercut opposition to the expansion of FBI power. Prostitution cases offered a similar opportunity. In 1910 Congress had passed the White Slave Traffic (Mann) Act, making it a federal crime to transport unmarried women across state lines for illicit sexual purposes. Responding to moralistic concerns that innocent farm girls, attracted to the glamorous life of the city, were then seduced into becoming prostitutes, and that local police officers could not cope with this serious moral problem, Congress through the Mann Act expanded the definition of interstate commerce crime and thereby the Bureau's law enforcement responsibilities. Although the legislation was intended to curb organized prostitution, it also made it a federal crime for an unmarried couple to travel to another state and then engage in sexual intercourse in a hotel or private residence.

Under Hoover's direction, the number of Mann Act cases brought by the Bureau increased from 377 in 1917 and 431 in 1922 to 524 in 1929—at a time when the number of Bureau agents declined from a wartime high of 579 in 1920 (having been 300 in 1917) to 441 in 1924 and then to 326 in

1932. Mann Act cases commanded public interest and for moralistic citizens confirmed the Bureau's value and professionalism. But the upsurge of these cases also prompted a critical response from many traditional conservatives who, during the 1930s, worried about the expansion of federal powers under the New Deal. The conservative editor of the *New York Daily News*, J. M. Patterson, for one, condemned as "a convenient instrument for blackmail" the FBI's highly publicized raids during the late 1930s which resulted in the arrests of hundreds of male customers of houses of prostitution, including a number of influential politicians, in Miami, Atlantic City, Philadelphia, and Trenton, New Jersey.

As with obscenity, Hoover's interest in prostitution was not limited to law enforcement. FBI agents were directed to monitor and report on illicit sexual activities even when no federal law violation had occurred or when the acquired information did not warrant referral to the U.S. attorney for possible prosecution.

Given the sensitivity of such reports and the fact that FBI records have not yet been turned over to the National Archives, we cannot determine how many Mann Act investigations initiated by the FBI resulted in prosecutions or referrals for prosecution. But indirect evidence suggests that most of the FBI's Mann Act investigations did not result in prosecution, and that this was a purposeful result of Hoover's motives in obtaining information about sexual liaisons.

Hoover refused to turn over FBI records to the National Archives, claiming that public access would impair the

FBI's ability to meet its law enforcement responsibilities (by enabling criminals and spies to learn Bureau methods and strategies). Thus by the 1940s he confronted a major housekeeping problem: the steadily accumulating records threatened to overwhelm available space. In 1944 Hoover ordered a review of the Bureau's closed Mann Act investigation files covering the years 1912–1919. FBI records personnel advised the FBI director that these records no longer had current value but did contain "considerable information of a very personal nature and potentially damaging to the character of the person" who had been the subject of the investigation. The FBI supervisor conducting this review thereupon drafted a proposed plan to destroy these records subject to the approval of the National Archives. (Under federal records law the National Archives has the responsibility to preserve federal records of "historical value.") When Archives officials rejected the FBI plan and proposed instead to accession these records because of their research value to historians and sociologists, Hoover withdrew the plan. If these records were to "perchance become, even in part, public property," the FBI director was advised by his Records Management Division, the FBI would find itself "in an embarrassing position without even the defense of an indictment or authorized complaint."*

*This 1944 decision not to turn over dated records to the National Archives postponed the resolution of the worsening housekeeping problem. In 1950 FBI Assistant Director Louis Nichols proposed an alternative solution: microfilming all Bureau records for the 1908–1922 period and destroying the bulkier originals. The only other alternative, Nichols advised Hoover, would be "turning them over to [National] Archives which could be suicidal."

The collection of such noncriminal information had not been inadvertent; nor was it the case that Mann Act investigations simply failed to develop sufficient information to warrant prosecution. This is indirectly confirmed by a special records procedure Hoover devised in 1949 to address the problem of "facts and information which are considered of a nature not expedient to disseminate, or which would cause embarrassment to the Bureau if distributed" outside the FBI. Henceforth agents were to report such embarrassing information not in the texts of their reports but on the administrative page appended to the report. Whenever the report was distributed outside the FBI, the administrative page could be detached without the recipient knowing that information was being withheld. After describing the rationale for this new reporting procedure, Hoover offered specific examples of the type of information to be submitted on administrative pages:

> During the legal search in a White Slave Traffic Act investigation there is found an address book containing data identifying prominent public officials. Unless the names appearing therein are material to the investigation, this type of information should be placed in the administrative section.
> An anonymous complaint alleges A ... is a member of the Communist Party and further that A is a man of lax morals, a heavy drinker living with a known prostitute. On the basis of other information in the [FBI's] files a case is opened [on individual A].

The allegation of Communist Party membership should be included in the investigative section while the allegation concerning loose morals should be included in the administrative section.

Hoover's contrasting examples highlight his interest in illicit sexual activities, whether of prominent politicians or radical activists. This was not mere voyeurism; it reflected an astute understanding of the potential value of such information. Noncriminal sexual information could later be used at an appropriate time, with both the timing and method of dissemination determined by the cautious FBI director.

OSTENSIBLY to further the FBI's liaison program with members of Congress, Hoover devised a system to identify those congressmen who would be friendly to the FBI and those who would not. This effort began on an informal, ad hoc basis in the 1940s, but by the 1950s it had evolved into a formal program. "Summary memoranda" were compiled on prospective congressional candidates, to supplement those already collected on incumbent members. Maintained in a safe but centralized depository (first in the Records Unit and later in the Administrative Unit), these memoranda could be consulted for background information on a member of Congress.

To prepare these summaries, FBI field offices were to

forward all information they had amassed on an individual—from newspapers and biographical sources or "any information the field office might have in its files." This submission was to be done either orally or by "informal written" memoranda (and, when submitted in writing, not by cover letter but by routing slip). The field office information was then supplemented by whatever information was retained in headquarters files on the individual to create a comprehensive summary.

This informal submission procedure created no official record that field offices had submitted information on congressional candidates, or that headquarters had retained it. Thus Hoover could deny that the FBI investigated and maintained files on members of Congress. No such files were serialized and indexed in the FBI's central records system. No retrievable records indicated that FBI field offices were required to forward (and did forward) information on members of Congress. These safeguards were essential precautions, for the information in the "summary memoranda" included "allegations of criminal or corrupt practices, subversive activities, and immoral conduct."*

---

*In the 1960s Hoover extended this formal reporting procedure to governors and gubernatorial candidates. In addition, he instructed his aides regularly to prepare similar summaries on presidential candidates and their key advisers—as reflected in the following four examples. On July 13, 1960, the date John F. Kennedy won the Democratic presidential nomination, Hoover's aides prepared a summary memorandum listing all the derogatory personal and political information that the FBI had amassed on Kennedy (including his World War II affair with Inga Arvad; that in January 1960 he had been " 'compromised' with a woman in Las Vegas"; and that he had been "involved in parties in Palm Springs, Las Vegas and

Hoover's practice was inadvertently disclosed in September 1972, after his death and owing to a careless communication by his successor, L. Patrick Gray. Confronted with the revelation, senior FBI officials benignly described these reports as simply designed to promote better liaison, to determine whether or not a member of Congress would support the FBI. Other FBI officials, however, rebutted this rationale. In an interview with *Los Angeles Times* reporter Jack Nelson, former FBI Assistant Director William Sullivan* described Hoover as a "master blackmailer. The moment he would get something on a senator he would send one of the errand boys up and advise the senator that

---

New York City" with *Confidential* magazine having "affidavits from two mulatto prostitutes in New York"). FBI officials also prepared summary memoranda on Democratic presidential candidate Adlai Stevenson, doing so on April 3, 1952 (when Stevenson's name was first mentioned as a possible Democratic candidate), on July 24, 1952 (when Stevenson belatedly agreed to allow his name to be submitted for nomination at the Democratic National Convention), and on March 22, 1956 (when Stevenson again sought his party's nomination). "In anticipation" of Henry Cabot Lodge's nomination as the Republican vice-presidential candidate, a summary memorandum on him was prepared on July 28, 1960. Finally, owing to Dwight Eisenhower's lack of a political past before he won the Republican presidential nomination in 1952 (he had no known party affiliation or positions on most public policy issues), Hoover instructed his aides that August to prepare summaries on Eisenhower's key campaign staff advisers (Leonard Hall, Wayne Hood, Wesley Roberts, and Robert Humphreys). When Roberts was selected by the successful president-elect as chairman of the Republican National Committee, Hoover ordered "a check made at once to find out if anything on Roberts since check made in Aug. 1952."

*Sullivan was forced to retire in September 1971 over differences in policy that had caused Hoover to question his loyalty. At the time, Sullivan held the number three position in the FBI hierarchy as assistant to the FBI director.

we're in the course of an investigation and by chance happened to come up with this data on your daughter.* But we wanted you to know this—we realized you'd want to know it. Well, Jesus, what does that tell the senator? From that time on, the senator's right in his pocket."

Hoover's alleged uses were described more colorfully by a former FBI agent during 1975 testimony before the House Select Committee on Intelligence Activities. He had been puzzled by this practice of compiling information on members of Congress, the former agent testified, so he and another agent had sought an explanation from their immediate supervisor, FBI Assistant Director Cartha DeLoach. The former agent quoted DeLoach's response:

> "You fellows have been in the Bureau for more than 10 years, so I guess I can talk to you off the record." He said, "The other night we picked up a situation where this Senator was seen drunk, in a hit-and-run accident, and some good-looking broad was with him." He said, "We got this information, reported it in a memorandum" and DeLoach—and this is an exact quote—he said, "By noon of the next day the good Senator was aware we had the information and we never had any trouble with him on appropriations since."

---

*Sullivan's example was not hypothetical. Having learned about the anti–Vietnam War activities of Congressman Henry Reuss's daughter, who was then a student at Swarthmore College, Hoover had one of his agents brief the congressman. In this case Reuss was unimpressed, for he supported his daughter's political activities.

The FBI's summary memorandum file has not been released, and may no longer exist. After its inadvertent disclosure in 1972, FBI officials considered destroying it on the premise that these were not "official" records and thus not subject to the records retention provisions of the Federal Records Act. And Hoover's procedure specified that summary memoranda were not to be retained once the member of Congress was defeated for reelection or retired from office. But whatever records remain would not be retrievable under the Freedom of Information Act. That act exempts from disclosure records pertaining to a living person; and if the person is deceased, it permits the withholding of derogatory personal information. Even if they were fully released, the summary memoranda would not reveal how Hoover and FBI officials had used this information. Hoover would have had no reason to create records of such actions. Any documentation of his interest and use would have been maintained in the secret files he kept in his office. One of these files, Hoover's Official and Confidential File, provides isolated examples of his interest in and use of summary memoranda. A far more comprehensive record of Hoover's actions has already been destroyed—the massive Personal and Confidential File that his administrative assistant, Helen Gandy, shredded in the month after Hoover's death in May 1972. In his "personal" file was stored the most sensitive information acquired about members of Congress.*

*This is indirectly documented by the concluding sentence of a summary memorandum prepared in 1971 on Senator George McGovern. Assuring FBI Assistant Director Thomas Bishop of the comprehensiveness

One of the existing folders from Hoover's Official and Confidential File shows how the FBI director was involved in such information. It contains a summary memorandum on former Massachusetts senator Henry Cabot Lodge, Jr. Begun in November 1946, this summary was updated periodically and focused on Lodge's political activities and policy positions as well as his contacts with the FBI and with Hoover. The summary also included reports that in 1922 Lodge had been arrested and "charged with intoxication" and in 1943 had been ticketed for a parking violation. In 1952 a more damning entry was added: "Senator Henry Cabot Lodge was an alleged homosexual." This new information was recorded without any attempt to determine its veracity. In this instance, this information was never circulated.

Lodge had played a crucial role in promoting Dwight Eisenhower's nomination as the Republican candidate and in his election to the presidency in 1952. That fall, however, he was defeated in his own bid for reelection to the Senate. To reward Lodge for his help, Eisenhower nominated him as U.S. ambassador to the United Nations. Yet because the president-elect sought to publicize his administration's greater vigilance in security matters, in contrast to the "laxity" of the exiting Truman administration, all his appointees, even those at the cabinet rank, were required to undergo FBI security clearance investigations.

---

of his search for all derogatory information on McGovern, FBI supervisor Milton Jones reported: "A review of the *personal records in the Director's Office* [emphasis mine] failed to locate any additional pertinent material concerning McGovern."

74

In the course of preparing the requested report on Lodge, FBI officials for the first time evaluated the allegation of homosexuality. A perfunctory review quickly established its implausibility. The source of the allegation was a homosexual in the military service who had bragged about his various homosexual associates. When questioned by military intelligence officers, the recruit admitted to having made false statements concerning his homosexual relations with Lodge and other prominent officials "for the purpose of impressing people." He had also named Franklin Roosevelt, Dean Acheson, Harry Hopkins, and Jesse Larson. For the first time the FBI evaluated this admission and in "the absence of any indication of homosexuality of Lodge being discovered during current [FBI] investigation," FBI Assistant Director Louis Nichols recommended to Hoover that the homosexual allegation "not be disseminated" in the FBI's report on Lodge to Sherman Adams, assistant to the president.

A second example involved a case of greater personal concern to Hoover. In public testimony in 1970, Hoover both impugned the loyalty of Catholic peace activists Daniel and William Berrigan and claimed that these priests were involved in a conspiracy to kidnap President Nixon's national security adviser, Henry Kissinger. Tennessee Congressman William Anderson responded by publicly condemning Hoover's abuse of office in accusing these peace activists without first seeking a criminal indictment. In an attempt to curry favor with the incensed FBI director, Memphis SAC James Startzell reminded Hoover that the

Memphis office had uncovered information on Anderson's "personal habits and morality," specifically that he allegedly consorted with prostitutes during visits to his congressional district.

Hoover welcomed this unsubstantiated allegation— "what a whore-monger this old reprobate is!"—and thanked Startzell for his "thoughtfulness." Then, to defame Anderson's reputation and to shore up the Nixon administration's hasty effort to quell this public furor by seeking a grand jury indictment of the Berrigans on the kidnaping charge, Hoover relayed this report "concerning Congressman Anderson's alleged extracurricular activities" to Nixon White House aide H. R. Haldeman, Attorney General John Mitchell, and Vice President Spiro Agnew. "The Bureau has conducted no investigation regarding this," Hoover wrote, "as no Federal violation appears to be involved." Nonetheless, he thought the recipient officials would be interested in gaining "some insight into the character of the man."

For this sort of quiet character assassination, Hoover did not depend on the thoughtfulness of SACs throughout the country but capitalized on the uniquely placed resources of the FBI's Washington, D.C., field office. Relying on wiretaps, bugs, the cooperation of the Washington police, and interviews with known prostitutes and hotel officials, FBI agents in the Washington area were able to report to an interested FBI director the alleged sexual indiscretions of, and other derogatory information about, the nation's lawmakers. Foreign diplomats, White House aides, cabinet officials, and businessmen also received attention. Hoover "deeply" appreciated "the benefit of this information," when he learned that a senator was an alcoholic and had recently been released from Bethesda Naval Hospital; that the wife of a congressman had been having an affair with a House Post Office employee; that a married senator had been "living with" a "party girl" at the Shoreham Hotel; that a local prostitute had had "sexual intercourse with a Senator during the afternoon 'on the couch in the Senator's office' "; that another prostitute had "$100 prostitution dates" with a governor, a senator, and six congressmen (one of whom "wanted her to perform unnatural sex acts with him" and also took "nude photographs" of her); and that a homosexual prostitute had a long-term relationship with a senator and had "obtained in excess of $2,000 in cash from the Senator during their association."*

How Hoover used this information is unclear. His interest, in any event, was not voyeuristic. The reports confirmed Hoover's personal interest in and the FBI's purposeful collection of derogatory information about members of Congress and other prominent Washingtonians. Because of their political sensitivity, no carbon copies were made, and they were kept in Hoover's secret Official and Confidential File. This assurance of secrecy enabled Hoover to determine when and how to use the information. Two contrasting examples of Hoover's tactics involve an attempt by conservatives to publicize the extramarital affairs of

---

*The various individuals were identified by name in these reports; the FBI withheld their names when it processed my Freedom of Information Act request.

Michigan Senator Arthur Vandenberg, and a sensitive request from President Lyndon Johnson.

As a dark-horse candidate for the Republican presidential nomination in 1948, the politically conservative Vandenberg was opposed by the isolationist wing of the Republican party because he had supported ratification of the United Nations Charter in 1945 and the Truman administration's aggressive containment policy in 1947–1948. As part of an effort to submarine Vandenberg's candidacy, conservative activists tried to impugn his reputation by documenting his suspected extramarital affair with Betsy Robertson, whom they identified as an "agent of the British Foreign Service who had been sent to the United States for the specific purpose of contacting Vandenberg and obtaining information about him." When he was briefed about this alleged affair in early June 1948, Hoover also learned of an elaborate plan of Frank Waldrop, editor of the arch-conservative *Washington Times-Herald*, to discredit Vandenberg. Waldrop told FBI Assistant Director Louis Nichols that while he was briefly out of town, Bootsie Cassini's gossip column in the *Times-Herald* had mentioned an unnamed "prominent" politician and presidential aspirant who had been seen with his "paramour" at Washington's Union Station. This cryptic reference to Vandenberg's affair with Robertson, Waldrop said, had temporarily stymied the *Times-Herald*'s "project" to "obtain a photograph of Vandenberg entering or leaving the Robertson house."

Later that month conservative activists sought to use this information when lobbying delegates to the Republican

National Convention, claiming that the FBI had a "huge file" on the matter. Hoover moved quickly to avoid having the FBI brought into this party conflict. The FBI director ordered Nichols to brief the senator's son and campaign manager, Arthur Vandenberg, Jr., on Waldrop's planned strategy. Nichols also assured Vandenberg that the FBI had no file on his father. Thanking Nichols for this information, Vandenberg, Jr., asked whether FBI officials would publicly deny maintaining a file on his father. Nichols refused to do so because he was unwilling to allow the FBI to be drawn into this imbroglio, suggesting instead that the senator threaten his detractors with a libel suit if they continued to circulate this allegation.

Technically, Nichols's denial was truthful. Information about Vandenberg's affair was not maintained in the FBI's central records system. Hoover instead kept these reports in his office, indexed under the name of the senator's son. Moreover, Waldrop had not been the sole or even the first source of Hoover's awareness of Vandenberg's alleged womanizing: the FBI director had "received similar information from other sources in the past."

Although Hoover was unwilling to assist either Vandenberg's opponents or supporters, he was more than responsive to a 1964 request from President Lyndon Johnson. As he approached the mandatory retirement age of seventy, Hoover received a respite from the dreaded possibility that he might lose the FBI directorship when President Johnson, by a May 1964 executive order, waived this requirement for an unspecified period. The vulnerable FBI director thereafter serviced a number of questionable presidential requests—including dispatching a special FBI squad to the 1964 Democratic National Convention in Atlantic City to provide valuable political intelligence to the White House. Hoover was similarly responsive to another Johnson request. On October 14 the Washington, D.C., police vice squad apprehended Johnson aide Walter Jenkins in the midst of propositioning a retired military officer to commit a homosexual act. Fearful that his Republican opponent, Senator Barry Goldwater, might exploit the Jenkins matter in the waning weeks of the campaign, Johnson requested FBI name checks on all members of the senator's staff. On Hoover's "instructions," FBI agents reported back with derogatory information that one Goldwater aide "frequently dated prostitutes...in his office."

The Vandenberg and Johnson episodes offer contrasting examples of Hoover's willingness to use FBI-obtained information. It was in Hoover's interest to assist Johnson, but not Vandenberg. Yet in both cases the FBI director could decide whether to render assistance because the FBI had already collected derogatory information. Both cases highlight as well Hoover's interest in limiting knowledge about his possession and uses of such information. The diverse ways by which the FBI director acted on FBI reports about John F. Kennedy's alleged sexual affairs offer additional insights into his caution.

The most publicized of these reports involved Kennedy's wartime affair with Inga Arvad. FBI agents had inadvertently discovered this affair during an investigation in 1942 of

Arvad, who was at the time a gossip columnist for the *Washington Times-Herald.*

The impetus to this investigation was a charge by one of Arvad's colleagues that she was a German spy, and the fact that she was employed by a newspaper that before Pearl Harbor had denounced President Roosevelt's interventionist foreign policy and had been decidedly pro-German in reporting on developments in Europe. FBI agents never uncovered evidence to support the "espionage" allegation. A six-month investigation—which included physically following Arvad, closely reviewing her published columns, breaking into her apartment to photocopy her papers, and wiretapping her residence—established only that she held conservative and isolationist views. But the investigation did uncover her sexual liaisons with Kennedy and another suitor. When they were alerted through the wiretap of Arvad's plans to visit Kennedy in Charleston, South Carolina (where he was stationed in the navy), FBI officials arranged to bug her hotel room during two weekend visits. Thus they were able to confirm that Kennedy and Arvad (who at the time was married but was in the process of divorce) had "engaged in sexual intercourse on a number of occasions" and that Arvad had advised Kennedy during the second visit that she "was quite worried about becoming pregnant."

Because of the sensitivity of this 1942 investigation, the resulting reports were routed to FBI Assistant Director Louis Nichols's secret office file. This decision was not due to the discovery of the Kennedy-Arvad affair; that was a later consideration. It was because the records would confirm the FBI's monitoring of an employee of a major newspaper critical of the Roosevelt administration. Discovery of this investigation, Hoover and senior FBI officials then feared, might have harmful consequences. The publisher of the *Times-Herald* had already questioned whether the FBI was monitoring the administration's conservative press critics, and "it is believed . . . would be quick to expose any investigation of the FBI."

The Arvad file acquired a different character in July 1960. When Hoover was briefed on July 13 (the day Kennedy won the Democratic presidential nomination) on derogatory information about the candidate in FBI files, he was reminded of Kennedy's wartime affair with Arvad. The next day, July 14, the file on Arvad/Kennedy was transferred to Hoover's office.

Hoover did *not* convey to Kennedy, either during the ensuing presidential campaign or during his presidency, that he had information about the Arvad affair. That would have been politically suicidal. Hoover could not defend the FBI's acquisition of this personally compromising information as inadvertent—the by-product of a wartime espionage investigation. For the FBI's intensive investigation had uncovered no evidence of Arvad's alleged espionage activities. More damaging, when Hoover had learned from the Arvad wiretap that she suspected her phone was tapped and that she planned to contact the FBI about this matter, he immediately ordered the tap discontinued—only to reinstate it within two months at the direct request of President Roosevelt. Thus disclosure of the Arvad affair might have dire political consequences for Hoover. On the one hand, it would refute his self-proclaimed apolitical posturing by confirming his willingness to assist a liberal president's effort to discredit a conservative newspaper adversary. On the other hand, Kennedy's bachelor status and known courtship of Arvad at the time made it feasible for Kennedy to rebuff any FBI disclosure as an attempt to blackmail.

Hoover decided to use this same information at a more propitious time. During a February 7, 1975, appearance on NBC's "Today" show, former Nixon White House aide Charles Colson stated that the FBI had provided "extensive information to the White House in 1971 or 1972" concerning Kennedy's wartime affair with Arvad. Responding to press interest that followed from Colson's comment, FBI officials claimed that a search of the Arvad file "fails to indicate any data" that Kennedy's affair with Arvad "was ever disseminated by the FBI either orally or by memorandum at anytime including the White House in 1971 or 1972 as implied by Mr. Colson."

The Arvad file in fact contains no memorandum of any such oral or written briefing. But this does not mean that no briefing occurred. From its creation in 1942, the Arvad file had been held either in Nichols's or Hoover's office as a tightly controlled secret. Colson could only have learned of the investigation from the FBI director's office, and Hoover would have had no reason to create a record that FBI officials had orally briefed or had allowed Colson to review this file.

Hoover's likely briefing of Colson in 1971 was intended

to further the partisan interests of President Nixon. Its intended target was not John Kennedy but his younger brother, Senator Edward Kennedy, who was at the time feared by the Nixon White House as the president's strongest Democratic challenger.

Hoover's handling of the Arvad material was consistent with his willingness to confront President Kennedy directly about another Kennedy affair, this time with Judith Campbell. In March 1962 FBI officials briefed Hoover about their discovery—from wiretaps of organized-crime leaders John Roselli and Sam Giancana—of Campbell's associations with these crime leaders. Then, from a review of Campbell's "telephone toll calls," they reported that on four occasions in November 1961 and once in February 1962 she had contacted President Kennedy's secretary, Evelyn Lincoln. From other sources, Hoover was further advised, the FBI learned that Campbell was "the girl who was 'shacking up with John Kennedy in the East.' "

In this case Hoover could safely advise the president of the FBI's discovery, for the information had been obtained through an investigation of organized-crime leaders. The attorney general himself had authorized the Roselli and Giancana wiretaps. In a March 22 meeting with President Kennedy, Hoover told him of Campbell's associations with Roselli and Giancana. He did not, nor did he need to, add that he knew Kennedy was "shacking up" with Campbell. Hoover nonetheless remained interested in learning whether this affair continued. After March 1962 Campbell's associations were closely monitored, not only because of her association with Roselli and Giancana but because of her telephone contacts with Evelyn Lincoln and rumors of her having "had an affair with President Kennedy."

Hoover's methods were those of a subtle blackmailer—to convey only the FBI's ability to uncover sensitive, confidential information. One of Hoover's earliest reports to Attorney General Robert Kennedy about the president's alleged sexual relationships captures the cunning of his method. Hoover received from the FBI's office in Rome a copy of an interview with Alicia Purdom, published in the Italian weekly *Le Ore,* in which she claimed that her engagement to Kennedy in 1951 had been vetoed by the family because she was a Polish Jewish refugee. The FBI director immediately relayed this information to the attorney general. Because the source was a published interview, in an Italian newspaper no less, Hoover's action offered silent witness to the FBI's greater abilities to acquire even more damaging information within the United States. And because the volunteered information had been published, the attorney general could not question whether the FBI was monitoring his brother's activities.

The *Le Ore* and Campbell matters highlight both Hoover's interest in acquiring derogatory information and his use of it in circumstances that would not be challenging to the FBI. This is further documented by Hoover's handling of two other allegations involving the president's sex life.

In one case, a right-wing Washingtonian, Florence Kater, had tried from 1959 to publicize her claim that Kennedy had had an affair with Pamela Turnure, private secretary to his wife Jacqueline. Hoover closely monitored Kater's allegations and efforts to gain attention for her charge. But the FBI director did not advise the attorney general that the FBI had learned of these allegations until 1963, just after an article on Kater's allegation appeared in the white supremacist National States Rights party's newspaper *Thunderbolt*. Conveying the impression of having only recently discovered this matter, Hoover purposefully enclosed a copy of the issue of *Thunderbolt*.

The second case involved the inclusion of a biographical sketch of a woman named Malcolm Durie in a printed genealogy of the Blauvelt family. The sketch reported that Durie had at one time been married to John Kennedy, preceding his known marriage to Jacqueline Bouvier. Given Kennedy's Catholicism, this evidence of a secret "first marriage" might well affect his electoral prospects. Upon learning of this claim in 1961, FBI agents surreptitiously sought to confirm the reported marriage. An agent, "in a private capacity and without identifying himself as a Bureau agent," reviewed a copy of the Blauvelt genealogy at the New York Public Library, found the printed biographical entry, and forwarded a photocopy to Hoover. FBI agents also checked with a New Jersey attorney (the source of the Durie entry) who provided a more detailed account of the "first marriage." Kennedy had allegedly married Durie in 1939, had unsuccessfully filed for a Reno divorce in 1948, and had then obtained first a "sealed divorce" through the intercession of New Jersey's Democratic governor Robert Meyner in 1951, and then, through the quiet assistance of Boston's Archbishop Cushing, a Vatican annulment in 1953.

Having concluded that this detailed report was accurate, and having learned from another FBI contact that the right-wing *Manchester* (New Hampshire) *Union Leader* was checking into this story, Hoover now briefed the attorney general. During the course of a conversation involving official business, Hoover innocently inquired if the attorney general "had seen the story being circulated about the first marriage of the president." The attorney general replied that he had, dismissing the genealogical entry as erroneously based on a press report that Durie had once dated his brother. Continuing, Robert Kennedy said that Durie "used to go out with his [oldest] brother, Joe, and that the President, Jack, took her out once." The story being circulated was a "smear," Kennedy emphasized, but he thanked Hoover for bringing the matter to his attention. Taken by surprise by Kennedy's confident assurance—the attorney general had further remarked that he hoped the story would be published as the Kennedys could then sue for libel—Hoover brazenly expressed his personal outrage over the "anonymous" circulation of the rumor, adding that he had "just wanted him [Robert Kennedy] to be alert to this."

Hoover acted similarly when he found out about other of John Kennedy's sexual liaisons, notably those involving Alicia Purdom, Ellen Rometsch, Suzy Chang, Marie Novotny, an airline stewardess, and prostitutes in New York, Palm Springs, Las Vegas, and at a hospitality suite during the 1960 Democratic National Convention. In the case of the president's rumored affair with Marilyn Monroe, however, Hoover never even hinted that the FBI was amassing reports on these rumors. His sole action, consistent with his style of holding his cards close to his chest, came in July 1964 when he advised Robert Kennedy of a report that the attorney general had had an affair with Monroe and planned to divorce his wife in order to marry her. Because this allegation had recently been published in a book by right-wing activist Frank Capell, Hoover could safely apprise Kennedy of only this aspect of the FBI's accumulated information on the Kennedys' alleged sexual relationships with Monroe. Timing and proper circumstances were key considerations in Hoover's use of derogatory information on prominent officials; the FBI director was always fully aware that, unless he had a foolproof defense, a briefing might backfire on him and damage his continued tenure as FBI director.

Hoover's handling of derogatory sexual information on Eleanor Roosevelt again illustrates his astuteness. In February 1943 military intelligence officers assigned to the Counterintelligence Corps (CIC) made a dramatic discovery during their intensive surveillance of army air force recruit Joseph Lash, who was stationed at Chanute Air Force Base in Rantoul, Illinois. Monitoring Lash because of his pre-induction political activities, CIC agents intercepted his correspondence and telephone conversations with Mrs.

Roosevelt. When they found that Lash planned to meet with the First Lady over the weekend of March 5–7 in nearby Urbana, CIC agents followed his off-base movements. The next weekend, when Lash returned to Urbana for a weekend visit with his fiancée, Trude Pratt (who was married but in the process of obtaining a divorce), CIC agents not only followed Lash but bugged Pratt's hotel room and recorded their sexual activities. Later that month CIC agents monitored Lash's second weekend visit with Mrs. Roosevelt in Chicago. This time, however, hotel officials let the First Lady know that, presumably for security reasons, she had been under military surveillance. Upon returning to Washington, Mrs. Roosevelt protested to presidential aide Harry Hopkins about what she thought was unnecessary security. Hopkins, in turn, protested to Army Chief of Staff George Marshall who, on further inquiry, discovered the scope of CIC's domestic surveillance activities.

Incensed by this abuse of power, which also contravened the wartime delimitation agreement between the military services and the FBI,* Marshall reaffirmed the ban on CIC domestic surveillance and ordered the destruction of its domestic surveillance files. CIC officials concluded that this order came from President Roosevelt and that Lash's relationship with Mrs. Roosevelt was sexual, based on expressions of affection in her intercepted letters to Lash.

---

*Under this June 1940 agreement, the FBI was assigned exclusive responsibility for all investigations within the United States involving "subversive" activities. MID and ONI authority was restricted to military personnel.

They approached the FBI's liaison officer and offered to give him the file they had compiled on Lash and Mrs. Roosevelt. Believing the worst of the First Lady, Hoover accepted with alacrity this misinformation* and maintained it in his office indexed under the name of Joseph Lash.

If he was willing to receive derogatory information on Mrs. Roosevelt, Hoover was equally interested in ensuring that no one knew about it. When in 1949 *Washington Times-Herald* editor Frank Waldrop and then again in 1951 Republican Senator Arthur Watkins asked FBI officials if the Bureau had ever investigated the "Roosevelt-Lash incident," Hoover instructed his aides to find out whether knowledge of the incident came from someone in the FBI director's office. An inquiry established that this was not the case.** So Waldrop and Watkins (both conservative haters

---

*CIC agents had developed no evidence of a sexual affair between Mrs. Roosevelt and Lash, or of their further contention that President Roosevelt had been briefed on this alleged affair and had then sought to disband the CIC. The only CIC knowledge of Mrs. Roosevelt's affection for Lash came from her intercepted correspondence in which she expressed her endearment and concern for him. Yet the CIC also knew that during Lash's visits with Mrs. Roosevelt her personal secretary, Malvina Thompson, had been present, and that Mrs. Roosevelt provided moral support to Joseph Lash and Trude Pratt regarding their plans to wed and Pratt's hesitancy to seek a divorce out of concern for her children. The head of the CIC unit investigating Lash had urged his dismissal from the service, concluding from the intercepted correspondence that he was involved in a sinister New Deal conspiracy. To effect this objective, he recommended that Lash be arrested on a "morals charge" for his weekend tryst with Trude Pratt.

**FBI Assistant Director Louis Nichols reported that his investigation confirmed the loyalty of all the secretaries who had been privy to the receipt of this information from military intelligence or its inclusion in Hoover's office file.

of President and Mrs. Roosevelt) were informed that "there is nothing in the main [FBI] files" on this matter.

In 1949 and 1951, because President Truman was a New Deal Democrat and was himself under attack from Republican conservatives, Hoover did not dare confirm to Waldrop or Watkins that the FBI possessed such information. Waldrop and Watkins would undoubtedly have publicized the matter, with resulting damage to Hoover's continued tenure. The election of a Republican administration in November 1952 changed the political circumstances and offered the first opportunity for Hoover to use this misinformation to discredit Mrs. Roosevelt.

In January 1953 FBI Assistant Director Louis Nichols met with two conservative activists, George Murphy and Francis Alstock. Both had played important roles in the recent Eisenhower presidential campaign, and they were interested in advancing the anti-Communist cause in the aftermath of the election. Reporting to Hoover on this meeting, Nichols characterized Alstock and Murphy as "our type of people...both have blood in their eyes against the so-called pseudo-liberals." He added that they had volunteered to ensure that the "Bureau will have its man at the White House" who would "look out for our [FBI] interests." In the course of this conversation, Alstock and Murphy specifically praised Mary Lord's appointment as Mrs. Roosevelt's successor as U.S. delegate to the United Nations, identifying her as "our type of people" who would "have a desk at the White House." Alstock promised to "get her over here [to the FBI] in due time; that she could be very helpful." An impressed Nichols thereupon volunteered the derogatory information that the FBI had learned about Mrs. Roosevelt's "affair" with Joseph Lash. (Nichols did not display the file or confirm Hoover's personal possession of the material.) Alstock was not surprised. He reported Eisenhower's "thorough distrust, distaste and dislike" for Mrs. Roosevelt, adding that the president and Secretary of State John Foster Dulles wanted to "get her out of the picture." Welcoming Nichols's information, Alstock predicted that "as long as Eleanor was in the picture, she would not become the subject of any Congressional investigation, but that sooner or later there was going to be an investigation of her affair with Joe Lash."

FBI officials soon sought other means to discredit Mrs. Roosevelt. Not knowing whether Alstock and Murphy had briefed Eisenhower, in February 1954 Nichols remarked to Hoover that "the thought occurs" that the FBI director "might want to consider mentioning this incident to him." As a reason for doing so, Nichols pointed out that Lash was currently a reporter for the *New York Post,* that the editor of the *Post* and Mrs. Roosevelt had been critical of both the FBI and the Eisenhower administration, and that this derogatory information might thus be of interest to the president. Hoover created no record of having briefed Eisenhower, but it is likely that he did.

WHILE Hoover may have been willing to help the more sympathetic Republicans in advancing the anti-Communist cause, the new president was not immune from Hoover's scrutiny. Eisenhower's lack of a political past, and his recruitment as a candidate in the spring of 1952 led Hoover to check into the background of the candidate's closest political advisers. Then, following Eisenhower's election in November, Hoover concerted with Alstock and Murphy (as well as John Henshaw, *New York Herald-Tribune* publisher Ogden Reid, and syndicated columnist Fulton Lewis, Jr.) to promote more conservative internal security and foreign policies. Hoover was also interested in learning any derogatory information about the president, no matter the source.

In February 1954 the FBI director was briefed on a wiretap of John Vitale, whom FBI officials described as "a St. Louis hoodlum." In his conversation with a Detroit associate, Vitale had asked about finding a good attorney, one who had influence and not necessarily legal talent. Vitale's Detroit associate recommended Herbert Hyde, whom he said was "getting powerful all the time now that Hyde is the General Trial Attorney for General Services Administration." Anticipating Vitale's doubts about Hyde's ability to "have anything to do with what we want," Vitale's Detroit associate then explained the basis for Hyde's influence and the likelihood of his appointment as a judge: "he's [Hyde] got a good looking wife—he says that IKE [President Eisenhower] has been trying to get into her pants."

The report of this conversation, and the transcript of that portion concerning Eisenhower, was immediately relayed to Hoover and was thereupon filed in the secret office file of FBI Assistant Director Louis Nichols. It is unclear what uses Hoover made of this information. The FBI has withheld in its entirety the ten-page memorandum created in response to this discovery. Yet FBI officials' justifications for withholding this document provide insights as to its contents—that release of the information would (1) violate privacy rights, (2) reveal FBI sources and methods, and (3) compromise internal FBI rules and procedures. These justifications confirm that the FBI had checked into Hyde's background and had, under established policy, in some way acted on the information.

A second example involving Eisenhower's sexual activities highlights Hoover's willingness to receive such information even when the source was one of the president's political adversaries.

After the Army-McCarthy hearings in 1954, Senator Joseph McCarthy had become persona non grata at the White House. The senator, in turn, grew harsher in condemning the president's foreign policy and internal security procedures. Consistent with his hardball approach to politics, he also sought to discredit the president. In one such crude attempt, in May 1955, McCarthy's key aide Don Surine contacted FBI Assistant Director Louis Nichols to report "scuttlebutt" about Eisenhower's alleged wartime affair with Kay Summersby, and the further rumor that in 1944 Eisenhower had asked General George Marshall whether his military career would be adversely affected by a divorce. Nichols's report on Surine's allegation was duly filed. Four months later Surine recontacted Nichols "to confidentially advise that Kay Summersby, a former WAC

Staff Officer assigned to President Eisenhower [during World War II] in Europe, had been staying at the [Washington] Shoreham Hotel for the last 30 to 45 days under an assumed name."

Despite the fact that the source of this unconfirmed allegation was one of the president's political enemies, Hoover nonetheless demanded that his aides "see if we can discreetly get the [assumed] name." The effort went forward on several fronts. Nichols asked Surine for the name, explaining that his request "stems from personal curiosity and has no connection with the FBI." Surine was unhelpful. At the same time FBI officials compiled a detailed report on Summersby's background and personal life while trusted agents in the FBI's Washington, D.C., and New York field offices sprang into action. The Washington agents "made discreet check through contacts at Shoreham" and learned that "no individual is registered there" under Summersby's married or maiden names and that "other variances were checked out with negative results." New York agents made two "pretext calls" to Summersby's New York residence but were equally unsuccessful—"no information received which would indicate whether she had recently been in Washington or not." Reporting the results of this unsuccessful inquiry to Hoover, Nichols assured him that "All checks mentioned above were made with complete secrecy and it is felt that no interest has been aroused on the part of outsiders concerning this matter."

Because Surine's report could not be verified, no use could be made of his information. Still, Hoover adopted additional safeguards to ensure that his interest in and the FBI's attempt to verify Eisenhower's sexual misconduct could not become known. In striking contrast to the Eleanor Roosevelt, John Kennedy, and Arthur Vandenberg allegations, both the Vitale and Surine reports alleging Eisenhower's sexual misconduct were kept in Nichols's secret office file, not Hoover's.* The FBI director realized that discovery of his interest in such information about Eisenhower could undermine his support among Republicans who had otherwise tolerated his behavior toward liberal Democrats.

THAT Hoover was interested in information about *any* prominent political leader could have precipitated bipartisan demands for his dismissal. Yet when the subjects of reported sexual misconduct were less privileged, and were also his political adversaries, Hoover responded more aggressively. A case in point involved his campaign against the influential civil rights leader Martin Luther King, Jr.

Hoover had suspected King's loyalty since his leadership role during the Montgomery bus boycott of 1955, and FBI

---

*Hoover had adopted this same procedure for filing the contemporaneous reports on the Arvad investigation. The additional safeguard of maintaining such records in Nichols's office file during the 1940s and 1950s allowed Hoover to deny that he personally maintained any records documenting FBI surveillance of employees of a conservative newspaper. This denial could similarly be repeated in Eisenhower's case—in the event that Surine or McCarthy claimed that the FBI had a "file" on Eisenhower's alleged affair with Summersby.

THE POLITICS OF SEX

agents closely monitored King's political and personal activities. Through contacts with Southern police officers, FBI wiretaps of King's residence and office, and FBI bugs of King's hotel rooms during his frequent trips around the country, Hoover learned about the civil rights leader's sexual activities—including recordings from the buggings of King's hotel rooms. Disclosure of these activities might impugn King's character and national reputation as a clergyman. Hoover maintained this information until the fall of 1964.

When King publicly criticized the FBI's failure to investigate civil rights violations in the South, Hoover became incensed. He also knew from intercepted conversations that the civil rights leader disparaged the FBI director's leadership and politics. Hoover now moved aggressively to discredit King. Copies of transcripts recording King's sexual activities, reports that King was involved in a sex orgy, and a photograph of King leaving a motel in the company of a white woman were offered to reporters from the *Washington Post*, *Newsweek*, the *New York Times*, the *Los Angeles Times*, the *Chicago Daily News*, the *Atlanta Constitution*, and the *Augusta* (Georgia) *Chronicle*. These leaks did not produce the desired results, as none of the reporters filed stories using the proffered information. To the contrary, *Newsweek* reporter Ben Bradlee protested to Attorney General Nicholas Katzenbach about this leak operation. Katzenbach promised to handle the matter and flew to Austin, Texas (where Lyndon Johnson was on vacation) to brief the president. He would take appropriate action, Johnson assured his attorney general—and then LBJ briefed

Hoover on Bradlee's protest, alerting him to this reporter's untrustworthiness.

Temporarily stymied by this failed effort to discredit King, in December 1964 Hoover ordered FBI officials to prepare for future use transcriptions and summaries of "data" recording the "various incidents" of sexual activity intercepted through the bugging of King's hotel rooms. In one such use of this "data," FBI Assistant Director William Sullivan drafted an anonymous letter that was sent to King's home, addressed to Mrs. King, with enclosed taped excerpts from the recordings. This letter threatened to expose King for the "fraud" he was. "You are done," it said, and concluded by suggesting that King consider committing suicide:

> King, there is only one thing left for you to do [in the next thirty-four days before King was to receive the Nobel Peace Prize].... There is but one way out for you. You better take it before your filthy, abnormal fraudulent self is bared to the nation.

The intensity and boldness of Hoover's efforts to discredit King were atypical. But not Hoover's willingness to use derogatory personal information to discredit those whom he considered subversive. In the case of radical activists, no holds were barred—in part because the leaking of derogatory personal information about radical activists carried minimal political risk, given their pariah status during the cold war era. Just as important, conservative reporters and editors were more than willing to honor Hoover's condition for using this information—that they not disclose the FBI's covert assistance.

Derogatory information about the illicit sexual activities of prominent radicals was purposefully divulged as part of a code-named program (COINTELPRO) to "harass, disrupt or discredit" targeted radical organizations and their leaders. Anonymous letters were sent to the parents of New Left activists, reporting on their sons' or daughters' premarital sexual activities and use of illicit drugs. FBI officials prepared information for widespread distribution to reliable reporters on the "scurrilous and depraved nature of many of the [New Left] characters' activities, habits, and living conditions." When the resulting newspaper articles did not meet Hoover's expectations, SACs were chastised for ignoring the "mounting evidence of moral depravity" and were ordered to adopt a more aggressive approach to demonstrate the "depraved nature and moral looseness" of student radicals. *Chicago Tribune* reporters were leaked information about the "playboy activities" of a prominent black Communist and the "extra-marital relationship" of two other Communists. The wife of a white civil rights activist received an anonymous letter written by FBI agents in a way so as to convey the impression that its author was a black woman; the letter confided that the woman's husband, while away from home ostensibly working to advance civil rights, was having sex with black women. This ploy succeeded in breaking up an already troubled marriage. Anonymous agents telephoned unmarried radical activists in the middle of the night to question their moral character. And, in an extreme act of retribution, FBI agents hired prostitutes known to have venereal disease to infect New Left leaders on the premise that their contracting the disease would undermine the support of campus followers. In an earlier, more benign version of this tactic, FBI agents had hired prostitutes to entrap leaders of the Fair Play for Cuba Committee.

The pariah status of radical heterosexuals permitted this more aggressive politics of sex. Even so, the limits of such uses were abandoned in the case of homosexuals, regardless of their political orientation and status.

From 1937 Hoover had haphazardly collected information about homosexuals, but he had been able to use this accumulated information only in special circumstances. The heightened security concerns of the cold war years provided an opportunity both to rationalize the collection of such information and to use it more purposefully. The timing was triggered by Senator Joseph McCarthy's dramatic and ultimately effective criticisms of the Truman administration's internal security policies.

The Democratic leadership in the Senate was at first convinced that McCarthy lacked evidence to support his highly publicized February 1950 charges that the Truman administration had tolerated the presence of eighty-one known "Communists in the State Department." So the Democrats decided to create a special Senate committee to investigate these specified cases. Republican Senate leaders responded by encouraging McCarthy to press the matter, and they provided him with whatever evidence they could muster to make his charges seem credible. Nonetheless, the Republican leadership was reluctant to link the party's political fortunes to McCarthy's political assault because of his undistinguished career, relative obscurity, and lack of a national following.

The underlying purpose of the Democratic decision to investigate McCarthy's 81 cases had been to subvert what since 1949 had become a central feature of Republican strategy—discrediting liberal Democrats by questioning their loyalty and vigilance in safeguarding the nation's security from the Communist Menace. To sustain this politics while distancing themselves from McCarthy, Republican leaders at first focused on a related security issue. The same month as McCarthy's charges, the head of the Washington, D.C., police vice squad publicly asserted that at a "quick guess" 3,500 "sex perverts" were employed in the federal bureaucracy, of whom 300 to 400 were State Department employees. In response to this publicity, State Department security officers admitted that the department had fired 91 "sex perverts" since the establishment of the Federal Employee Loyalty Program in March 1947.

Prominent Republicans* moved quickly in April–May 1950 to exploit this security threat by sharply condemning the Truman administration's failure to root out "homosexuals in government." Republican National Committee

---

*These included Republican National Committee chairman Guy Gabrielson, Republican Senate whip Kenneth Wherry, and New York governor Thomas E. Dewey (who had been his party's presidential nominee in 1944 and 1948).

chairman Guy Gabrielson warned that "sex perverts who have infiltrated our government in recent years" were "perhaps as dangerous [a threat to internal security] as the actual Communists" whom McCarthy had cited.

Having lost the initiative because of Senator McCarthy's charges of Communists in government, the Truman administration now faced these allegations of homosexuality as well. The White House worked with the Democratic Senate leadership to undercut the concerns precipitated by these allegations. Owing to the sensitive personal privacy issues involved in examining the sexuality of federal employees, the special Senate committee established to investigate the problem of "homosexuals in government," chaired by North Carolina Senator Clyde Hoey, agreed to conduct its inquiry in secret, holding no public hearings. Nonetheless, when the committee released its report on this investigation in December 1950, it concluded that the employment of "sex perverts" posed a serious security problem, sharply criticized federal officials for having failed to take "adequate steps to get these people out of government," and demanded strict screening measures to prevent the further employment of homosexuals.

The committee's findings were not based on evidence that homosexuals had been blackmailed into betraying national secrets or were predisposed to commit espionage. The committee conceded that it had not uncovered any example of an American homosexual employee having betrayed national secrets. Nonetheless, its report endorsed the unsupported claims of U.S. intelligence officials that "sex perverts in government constitute security risks." Homosexuals should not be employed, these security officers asserted, because their "lack of emotional stability" and the "weakness of their moral fiber" rendered them "susceptible to the blandishments of foreign espionage agents."

Hoover quickly capitalized on this newly perceived internal security threat. In testimony before a House Appropriations Subcommittee in April 1951, the FBI director justified the substantial increase in the FBI's proposed appropriations as necessary to meet the greater investigative responsibilities mandated under the Federal Employee Loyalty Program. As evidence of both the increased danger and the FBI's vigilance, Hoover emphasized that FBI investigations had uncovered "derogatory" information on 14,414 of the 3,225,000 federal employees and applicants, and since April 1950 had successfully identified 406 "sex deviates" in government service.

Hoover succeeded in obtaining the increased appropriations. Then, on June 20, 1951, the FBI director unilaterally instituted a special Sex Deviates program "for furnishing information concerning allegations [of homosexuality] concerning present and past employees of any branch of the United States government." Under this program, information about sex deviates was to be disseminated to the White House and various federal agency boards; to "specific individuals" in both houses of Congress, the Government Accounting Office, the Library of Congress, the Government Printing Office, and the Botanical Gardens; and to a "specified individual" in the judiciary.

This code-named Sex Deviates program simply rationalized the FBI's ad hoc procedures formerly used to purge
homosexuals from government employment. Because FBI
officials succeeded in 1977 in obtaining the National
Archives' approval to destroy the massive files of the Sex
Deviates program, its scope and nature cannot be definitively
resolved, nor can the reliability of the FBI's reported evidence
of homosexuality be independently evaluated. The size of
the destroyed files—300,000 pages*—confirms the program's
massive proportions. Other existing FBI policy records verify
that the effort to purge homosexuals soon expanded beyond
federal agencies, and that the acquired information was
used for political purposes.

Although the specific files created for the Sex Deviates
program were destroyed, other FBI policy files recording
discussions of this and other FBI programs that disseminated
information outside the Bureau were not. Included among
these are memoranda reporting FBI officials' deliberations

*The FBI also created and maintains in its central records system an
unknown number of files captioned under the names of individuals and
organizations. Some of these records have been released and confirm the
scope of the Bureau's interest in homosexuals. Gays and lesbians were
spied upon, for example, in Los Angeles, San Francisco, Seattle, San Diego,
Denver, Chicago, New York, and New Haven. Organizations that were
specifically monitored included the Mattachine Society, the Daughters of
Bilitis, the Gay Activists Alliance, and the Gay Liberation Front. In
response to suits seeking such records, FBI officials denied that "homosexuals per se" had been monitored, claiming that "there would have to be
some indication that such activity would place the national security in
jeopardy." Yet the released files show that the individuals who were being
investigated had not been involved in defense work, nor had FBI agents
uncovered evidence of spying or other illegal activities.

over whether to continue or modify the FBI's ongoing dissemination programs. They confirm that Hoover had authorized the expansion of the Sex Deviates program beyond the federal bureaucracy. "In appropriate instances where the best interest of the Bureau is served," an October 1954 policy memorandum reports, "information concerning sex deviates employed either by institutions of higher learning or law enforcement agencies is disseminated to proper officials of such organizations." This memorandum then cites two examples of Hoover's approval of such dissemination: he personally "instructed" FBI officials in one case to "confidentially make available to George Washington University information concerning sex deviates or Communists employed there"; and in a second case he "confidentially" advised an FBI "contact" at New York University "as to the sex deviate practices of an instructor who was involved in the Police Training Field."

To effect this program, a special Sex Deviates card file was created. Each card listed the name of the individual, described his current occupation, and then identified the date and serial number and briefly summarized the specific FBI report leading to this listing—thereby ensuring that known homosexuals could be easily identified and that allegations of homosexuality (beyond those about federal employees) would not be lost within the FBI's massive case files. Although the index cards to this file were destroyed in 1977, one survived.

This card had been stored in Hoover's office file because of the sensitivity of its subject—Adlai Stevenson, then

Illinois governor and Democratic presidential nominee. The card identified Stevenson as governor of Illinois, thereby confirming that at least as early as April 1952 the Sex Deviates program was no longer confined to federal employees. The report resulting in Stevenson's listing further confirms that listings were not always based on corroborated information. The FBI's sources had been Bradley University basketball players (then under investigation for fixing basketball games) who had claimed that "The two best known homosexuals in the state [of Illinois] were [Bradley University] President [David] Owen* and Governor Stevenson, and that Stevenson was known as 'Adeline.' The basketball players were of the opinion that Stevenson *would not* run for President because of this."

Hoover's secret office file also offers tantalizing insights into how this (mis)information was used, and for what political purposes. The opportunity came in the month following Stevenson's selection as the Democratic presidential nominee. In August 1952, Milt Hill, who had been hired by the Republican National Committee to write the "official Republican biography of Governor Stevenson," contacted FBI Assistant Director Louis Nichols for help in verifying information Hill had received from a former FBI agent, Orval Yarger. Yarger's volunteered derogatory information focused on alleged corruption in the Illinois state purchasing department. Discussing this matter with Nichols, Hill observed that the Republicans "might get

---

*An index card on Owen had also been prepared, identifying him as the president of Bradley University.

someone after an investigation of these charges, to present the facts to the United States Attorney." Nichols quickly disabused Hill of this notion, pointing out that "the United States Attorneys are Democratics." Hill then sought verification of another of Yarger's charges, namely that Stevenson had been "arrested on a morals charge, put up bond, and elected to forfeit," and that was why Mrs. Stevenson "really divorced Stevenson."

Nichols immediately briefed Hoover about his meeting with Hill and Hill's partisan purpose. It remains unclear whether Hoover authorized Nichols to verify the homosexual allegation. Only the carbon copy of Nichols's memo to Hoover remains in Hoover's Official and Confidential File. The original more than likely had been filed in Hoover's more sensitive Personal and Confidential File; only it would have recorded Hoover's handwritten response on the bottom of the memo (the FBI director's method of responding to reported information). Nonetheless, other memoranda pertaining to this briefing, all of which involved far less sensitive matters than Yarger's homosexual allegation, confirm that Hoover had directed Nichols to determine the veracity of these other allegations. It seems likely, then, that Hoover also authorized Nichols to examine all FBI records pertaining to the homosexual allegation and then orally to brief Hill on their nature and reliability. Although they were unable to publish them in campaign literature, Republican campaign chiefs did circulate rumors of Stevenson's homosexuality.

The Sex Deviates card file later proved helpful in response

to an equally sensitive request from the Nixon White House. Having failed in its efforts to defeat incumbent liberal Democrats during the 1970 Senate elections by raising the "law and order" issue, the Nixon White House reassessed its strategy and shifted its attack to the objectivity of the Washington press corps. Vice President Spiro Agnew became the point man for this effort. As part of a strategy to discredit Washington-based reporters, White House aide H. R. Haldeman telephoned Hoover directly on November 25, 1970. As Hoover records it, Haldeman confided that the president "wanted him to ask, and he would imagine I [Hoover] would have it pretty much at hand so there would be no specific investigation, for a run down on the homosexuals known and suspected in the Washington press corps." Hoover confirmed that "we have some of that material." When Haldeman named a specific reporter (whose identity the FBI has withheld) "and some of the others rumored generally to be and also whether we had any other stuff; that he, the President, has an interest in what, if anything else, we know," Hoover agreed to "get after that right away."

Nixon correctly surmised that the FBI director need not initiate a special investigation to obtain this information. The Sex Deviates card file provided a readily retrievable system of identifying by name and occupation those individuals whose files contained reports of alleged homosexuality. Within two days Haldeman had Hoover's report.*

---

*Because Hoover was responding to a request from the Nixon White House, he created and preserved a record of this action. But in the

The Nixon request was atypical in its boldness and because of the targets of this White House attack. The normal procedure was for Hoover to volunteer derogatory personal information to the White House or responsible executive branch officials, either to effect the dismissal of certain individuals or whenever the FBI had uncovered "items with an unusual twist or concerning prominent personalities which may be of special interest to the President or the Attorney General." Such volunteered information included allegations that White House aides were homosexual.

The most dramatic such example involved Arthur Vandenberg, Jr., the son of the prominent Republican senator from Michigan and a key figure in Eisenhower's 1952 presidential campaign. As a reward for this assistance, and out of respect for Vandenberg's considerable political talents and contacts, Eisenhower appointed Vandenberg, Jr., White House secretary, a senior administrative position.

The president-elect required FBI security clearance investigations of all his appointees, so Vandenberg worried that the FBI might uncover his homosexual orientation. On December 16 he inquired of FBI Assistant Director Louis Nichols as to the progress of "his own investigation, stating

---

Stevenson matter, Hoover had no reason to preserve a record of his actions. On the contrary, he had every reason to destroy Nichols's original briefing memorandum, because the initiative came from Hill and not from a high-ranking official in the Eisenhower campaign. While Hoover did create a record of the date of his compliance with Nixon's request, he did not preserve a copy of his actual report. That report would have documented the scope of the FBI's monitoring of the sexual activities of prominent reporters.

he wished I [Nichols] would check into it as he was waiting for our report to come through in order to get away" for a vacation before helping to organize the new administration. He did not know "the exact status," Nichols responded, "but would check on it, that after all when an individual had traveled as far as [Vandenberg] had, it would take a little time." Nichols proposed that the two of them meet on December 20. At this meeting Vandenberg commented—seemingly innocently—that the president-elect wondered how the FBI "reported unfounded rumors." Nichols assured Vandenberg that whenever the FBI "picked up gossip and rumors, we checked them out and if definitely disproven, they were not included in reports, that, however, if they were the subject of widespread dissemination, they had a logical place being in the report because otherwise the reviewing officer would have no way of knowing whether they had been considered in the investigation if there was some future question." Apparently this response satisfied Vandenberg.

On December 23, however, Vandenberg entered a hospital in New York City, ostensibly for a physical checkup. He asked that the FBI "not interview the young man at present living with Vandenberg until he, Vandenberg, came out of the hospital." Vandenberg's concern stemmed from the fact that his roommate had recently been arrested on a homosexual charge, raising questions about Vandenberg's own sexual orientation. Briefed by Hoover on this development, Eisenhower instructed the FBI director that "should Mr. Vandenberg decide that he did not desire to continue in the position ... as Secretary to the President, that I [Hoover] could inform Vandenberg that no report would be submitted as it would be a moot question." Vandenberg was advised of this option, and upon his release from the hospital he announced that for health reasons he had decided not to accept the White House appointment. Holding to his end of the bargain, Hoover halted the FBI's security clearance investigation.*

Two developments in 1957 provide further insights into how Hoover both effected the dismissal of homosexuals and advanced the political interests of a favored administration.

In April of that year an employee in the White House mail room was arrested for having made an "improper approach" to a member of the Washington police vice squad. The Secret Service investigated and identified two other White House mail room employees also as homosexuals. In the course of questioning, one of the three

---

*Some years later, in discussing security clearance procedures with President-elect Richard Nixon's liaison, Henry McPhee, Hoover recommended that Nixon seek full FBI background checks of all proposed aides before announcing their appointments. As justification, the FBI director recounted President-elect Eisenhower's experience involving "one person appointed but not checked was to be a White House aide and had a bad record as a homosexual, and he was the son of a prominent Senator and when I told the President-elect about it, he was astounded." Hoover cited this example to confirm "the wisdom of getting these people checked [by the FBI] so that [the president and his advisers] can find any black shadow in the picture before they make a public announcement." Hoover also cited the case of President Johnson's aide Walter Jenkins, who had been "brought in" without "being checked by anyone, but Johnson vouched for him," and it ultimately became a "bad scandal as [Jenkins] was arrested" on a morals charge, much to the embarrassment of the Johnson White House.

admitted to having seen a confidential report on syndicated columnist Joseph Alsop's homosexuality and to having told his associates about it. At this point the White House referred the matter to the FBI as a possible security threat, fearing access to classified information by "associates of these three or others of the same propensities in other branches of the Government." The FBI never uncovered a sinister homosexual plot to betray classified information. After the investigation, the White House accepted the resignation of the three employees "due to the discovery of their involvement in homosexual activity."

Because of the discovery that a mail room employee had seen and discussed an FBI report on Alsop, Hoover immediately briefed Assistant to the President Sherman Adams on the "developments in the Joseph Alsop case." The FBI director noted that this "information [about Alsop's homosexuality] had been held quite closely." Only Attorney General Herbert Brownell and Deputy Attorney General William Rogers had been aware of this FBI report; Secretary of State John Foster Dulles, Under Secretary of State Christian Herter, and CIA Director Allen Dulles also had known of Alsop's admission to the CIA that he was homosexual and had been compromised by the Soviet police during a trip to Moscow.

A month before the arrest of the White House mail room employee, Hoover had prepared a summary memorandum on Joseph Alsop (and his brother Stewart). This was what the employee had seen. While the summary focused on the columnist's critical commentary on the FBI, it included a section reporting both the CIA information and the allegations of a former State Department employee. While stationed in Germany in 1954, this State Department employee alleged, he had met Alsop, who was then a house guest of a mutual friend, and Alsop had asked him to "obtain for him the services of a 'warmer' (homosexual)." Unable to locate a male prostitute, this informer admitted to having "finally engaged in a homosexual experience with Joe Alsop to satisfy Alsop's desires."

The FBI's interest in Alsop's activities had not begun only in 1957; it had been triggered by Joseph's (and his brother Stewart's) syndicated column. Between 1950 and 1955 the FBI conducted seven "leak" investigations of the Alsops "at the request" of the Justice Department and the Atomic Energy Commission, based on "unauthorized classified information appearing in their column." The Bureau had been unable to identify the Alsops' "source of information" because the classified information "published by them had been given wide-spread dissemination throughout the Government, in some cases to thousands of individuals in several departments and agencies."

Hoover's briefing of Adams, in any event, was triggered by a security concern that homosexual employees might have had access to FBI reports on homosexuals. The Alsop matter soon took a different twist. After the Soviets' dramatic success in launching Sputnik in 1957, and following the release of the controversial Gaither Report alleging the existence of a "missile gap" between the United States and the Soviet Union, Joseph Alsop published a series of columns criticizing the Eisenhower administration's reductions in defense appropriations as having led to Soviet missile superiority. In the process the columnist became a thorn in the side of the administration. In April 1959 Attorney General Rogers (who had succeeded Brownell) telephoned Hoover to express his surprise that Secretary of Defense Neil McElroy "did not know about the Joseph Alsop incident in Russia where Alsop admitted to certain acts of homosexuality." Rogers asked Hoover to put together "what we have on Alsop as he [Rogers] believed very few people knew of this and he was not sure that the President was aware of it." (Rogers did not know that in 1957 the White House had received an FBI briefing on Alsop.) Hoover agreed to prepare the summary, to which Rogers responded that "he was going to see that certain individuals were aware of Alsop's propensities, namely, The President, Secretary of Defense McElroy, Under Secretary of State Herter, [White House aide Wilton] Persons and Secretary to the Cabinet [Robert] Gray, ... but he would not take responsibility for such information going any further." It is unclear what uses Eisenhower administration officials made of this derogatory information, though Rogers's purpose was decidedly hostile.

ALTHOUGH Hoover was moralistic and judgmental, he had more than a personal interest in collecting and disseminating information about illicit sexual conduct. His purposes were, in a basic sense, political—whether in promoting a moralistic political climate or soliciting FBI reports on sexual misconduct and then surreptitiously divulging this information. Prominent personalities, radical activists, homosexuals—Hoover never tried to blackmail these individuals directly. Such crude tactics might backfire and provoke tighter restrictions on FBI activities or Hoover's own forced resignation as FBI director. His preferred method was to operate behind the scenes, relying on the covert but witting cooperation of members of Congress, reporters, and sympathetic officials in the executive branch who shared his immediate political objective.

THREE

The Politics
of Crime

H OOVER'S ability to acquire information about illicit sexual activities was a double-edged sword. Having this compromising information provided him leverage and thus enhanced his power. But the ambitious FBI director could never advertise the FBI's possession and use of such noncriminal information. For despite his initial success in refurbishing the image of a scandal-ridden Bureau, most Americans continued to believe that a federal police force could threaten privacy rights and monitor dissent. They valued the libertarian and states rights' principles underpinning constitutional amendments that barred "unreasonable" searches and seizures; prohibited laws "abridging freedom of speech or of the press, or the right of the people peaceably to assemble and to petition the Government for a redress of grievances"; reserved to the states "the powers not delegated to the United States by the Constitution"; and limited executive powers to "take care that the Laws be faithfully executed." Only with the political crisis of the Great Depression, an economic downturn that discredited laissez-faire, probusiness policies, were these formidable constraints overcome.

Changing politics ushered in the electoral victory of Franklin Roosevelt in 1932 and the enactment of New Deal legislation that expanded federal regulatory powers and responsibilities. No longer did most Americans believe that the best government was the least government, that the private sector alone should make labor, production, and investment decisions, and that only private charities and local and state governments should relieve the unemployed and the disadvantaged. The magnitude of the economy's collapse and the seeming inability of business leaders to ensure economic recovery made Americans more willing to sanction an increase in federal powers. To a frustrated public, Franklin Roosevelt's New Deal offered a hope of recovery and confirmed the value of a stronger federal government.

Yet fears of centralized power remained. To many conservatives, the New Deal posed a triple threat: New Deal agencies encroached upon formerly sacrosanct property rights, challenged the principle of personal responsibility, and undermined a government system of limited powers. At the same time Roosevelt's popularity and success in exploiting the media (through biweekly press conferences and nationwide radio addresses) to advance his legislative and spending proposals seemed to demonstrate the loss of citizen control over government policy and the advantages that high-profile federal officials commanded in any contest to shape public opinion.

This changed political setting shaped Hoover's response in exploiting a politics of crime. For a crime crisis had accompanied the collapse of the economy in the aftermath of the stock market crash in 1929—dramatized by highly publicized kidnapings and bank robberies and the apparent inability of local and state police to contain criminals.

The enactment of Prohibition did not command total public support during the 1920s as highly organized gangs profitably serviced a continued demand for alcoholic beverages. This lucrative business led to warfare between criminal gangs and between gangsters and outmanned local police, elevating public interest in curbing gangsterism. Hollywood both capitalized on and promoted these concerns of a worried citizenry, in 1931 alone producing more than fifty gangster movies. The kidnaping of the infant son of famed aviator Charles Lindbergh on March 1, 1932, symbolized the pervasiveness and seriousness of the crime problem—even national heroes were not immune, and the local police proved unable to solve this complex case. Simultaneously, a spate of bank robberies—dramatized by John Dillinger's successes in robbing ten banks between May and October 1933 and then avoiding capture or escaping from prison—strengthened support for federal action.

Franklin Roosevelt's new administration moved quickly to exploit these crime concerns. In mid-September 1933 the president publicly ordered Hoover to take control of the still unsolved Lindbergh case. In his annual address to Congress on January 3, 1934, FDR represented crime as a threat to "our security." "These ... violations of ethics," the president warned, "call on the strong arm of Government for their immediate suppression; they call on the country for an aroused public opinion."

In July 1933 Roosevelt's attorney general, Homer Cummings, announced that the Justice Department was drafting legislation to "arm" the nation against the upsurge of crime and proposed to extend federal jurisdiction over kidnaping, bank robberies, and extortion. Through biweekly press conferences and by hiring Henry Suydam (the Washington bureau chief of the *Brooklyn Eagle*) as a special assistant to handle the department's press relations, Cummings sought to ensure an "aroused public opinion." He did not shy from alarmist rhetoric, claiming that "Racketeering has got to the point where the [federal] government as such must take a stand and try to stamp out this underworld army." "The safety of our country," Cummings warned, was being threatened by the "organized forces of crime," and because crime was often "conducted by interstate gangs who operated across State lines," traditional remedies no longer worked. "State prosecution was breaking down. The police of the great cities were hopelessly corrupt. The rural system of crime control which was lodged in the sheriff and the constable was unsuited to modern conditions. If the elements of an offense were not all committed in a single State, such criminals might sometime escape prosecution altogether."

As part of his strategy, the attorney general pointedly extolled the professionalism and superior crime-fighting abilities of Hoover's FBI—promoting the image of the efficient, disciplined G-man (government agent, a term allegedly uttered by gangster George "Machine Gun" Kelly at the time of his arrest by FBI agents). This was accomplished through highly publicized FBI raids leading to the apprehension or killing of gangsters such as Kelly, Dillinger, Alvin "Creepy" Karpis, the Barkers, Harry Brunette, and Louis "Lepke" Buchalter.

But the FBI director was not interested simply in promoting legislation to expand federal law enforcement authority. His purposes were both more ambitious and narrowly bureaucratic: to establish the FBI's usefulness and at the same time avoid identifying the Bureau's growth and his own leadership as simply another product of the New Deal. Thus Hoover's strategy portrayed the crime crisis not in political terms—as a federal responsibility—but in moralistic, personalist, and technocratic terms. FBI press releases decried the stealth, cowardice, and brutality of gangsters and stressed the high ethical standards and traditional values of FBI agents. Downplaying the expansion of federal powers, the Bureau was depicted as scientific and technologically driven. This strategy of personalizing the crime problem as a conflict between the forces of good and evil, and of extolling his own and FBI agents' apolitical and scientific methods, focused attention on the apparent moral breakdown of modern society.

Hoover also did not simply rely on the Justice Department's public relations efforts. He developed his own staff under the direction of FBI Assistant Director Louis Nichols (and his successors, Cartha DeLoach and Thomas Bishop).

Hoover also capitalized on the contacts and skills of freelance writer and former reporter Courtney Ryley Cooper. In a mutually beneficial relationship, Hoover opened FBI files to Cooper, who then wrote a series of popular articles and books promoting the FBI's successes and the seriousness of the crime problem, notably *Ten Thousand Public Enemies, Here's to Crime,* and *Designs in Scarlet.* Cooper also ghostwrote Hoover's anticrime book *Persons in Hiding* and a series of Hoover-bylined articles in *American Magazine* that praised the FBI's role in fighting gang crime, combating the use of motels for illicit sexual liaisons, and (later in the 1930s) safeguarding the nation from spies and saboteurs.

Cooper brought to this writing assignment an ability to convey in a punchy and dramatic manner the seriousness of the criminal threat, and then the expertise of FBI agents and their demanding boss. Given privileged access to FBI records, Cooper told an interesting and suspenseful story, one where FBI agents prevailed because of their moral superiority and disinterested professionalism under Hoover's apolitical and efficient leadership. FBI officials in turn closely monitored Cooper's drafts to ensure their accuracy and their emphasis on Hoover's and the FBI's successes. Hoover also exploited the willingness of Cooper and his editor at *American Magazine* to promote the FBI's bureaucratic interests. Thus, after obtaining an advance copy of a forthcoming *American Magazine* article by Donald Keyhoe and John Daly, "The Spies Are Laughing," which implicitly criticized the "handling of espionage and sabotage" by the U.S. government (and thereby the FBI), Hoover wrote

Cooper's editor, Sumner Blossom, to suggest that "the time has come when there is a very definite need for the further enlightenment of the public." The result was a Hoover-Cooper bylined article (published under the title "Stamping Out Spies") which described the FBI's vigilance and outlined how the public could help monitor spies and saboteurs. Earlier, when he learned that William Moran, the former head of the FBI's bureaucratic rival, the Secret Service, was negotiating with Blossom over a series of articles on the work of the Secret Service, the FBI director received Blossom's assurances that Moran "will not, under any circumstances write anything derogatory to Mr. Hoover or the Bureau."

Hoover also capitalized on the popularity of movies. By the mid-1930s Hollywood producers had shifted the focus of their films from gangsters to FBI agents. Seven different films were released in 1935 alone melodramatically recounting the exploits of FBI agents, the most notable of them Warner Brothers' *G-Man*, starring James Cagney. Through the years Hoover worked with Hollywood and television producers on shows glorifying the FBI—but on the conditions that he retain the right to approve the scripts, and that agents were to be portrayed as intelligent, devoted to family, and All-American role models.

Aware that press agentry alone could not put across this image of the mythical G-man, Hoover instituted strict rules governing the appearance, deportment, and personal conduct of FBI agents. FBI personnel were to keep in mind that "the public look upon the Bureau of Investigation of

the Department of Justice as a group of gentlemen," and
were warned that should they fail to "conduct themselves
in office as such, I will dismiss them." SACs were to report
on "the conduct" of all employees both "while on official
duty and after official hours"; were to consider the personal
appearance of prospective agents because "the impressions
made by Special Agents on the public have a great deal to
do" with promoting public cooperation; and were personally
responsible for "preventing and deterring" any "incidents of
misconduct of Bureau personnel" under their supervision.
Agents were required to "give due regard to their personal
appearance and presentability" and only "patronize hotels
of the better class." They were not to use the phrase
"interrogated rigorously" in their reports as this might
convey "the impression that some form of duress" had been
used. And they were to avoid "being involved in a situation
resulting in embarrassment to the Agent or the Bureau." In
order to project a consistent image, Hoover required all
FBI personnel to obtain his approval before giving public
speeches "which contain editorializing, predictions or comment on national problems or policies."

Thus what began as an attempt by the Roosevelt administration to expand the federal government's law enforcement
authority eventuated in a carefully orchestrated public
relations victory for Hoover and the FBI. Hoover's strategy
of demonizing gangsters and mythologizing agents, and of
depicting the crime crisis in moralistic terms, defused the
issues of centralization, bureaucracy, and demagoguery
inherent in the FBI's growth and his own self-promoted

visibility. Hoover was no faceless bureaucrat but a revered and accessible public servant—citizens were urged to call or write the FBI director personally. FBI agents did not threaten the privacy rights of American citizens but protected them from a dangerous underworld. The FBI's increased power had not come at the expense of the states; instead, through the FBI National Academy established in 1935 to train local and state police officers in modern crime-fighting techniques and strategies, the Bureau assisted local police in meeting their crime-fighting responsibilities.

This nonthreatening perception of the FBI also derived from its relatively limited growth: the number of agents increased from 326 in 1932 to only 600 by 1936. The real impetus to Hoover's power came later, during the twin crises of World War II and the cold war, when the number of FBI agents increased to approximately 900 by 1940, then to 5,000 by 1945, 7,000 by 1952, and 10,000 by 1972.

THIS dramatic increase stemmed from Hoover's success in exploiting wartime and postwar concerns about the internal security threat posed by foreign-dominated fascist and communist movements. An increased FBI presence was necessary to apprehend spies and saboteurs and to anticipate and frustrate the efforts of enemy spy agencies and their recruits. In the process, investigating criminals became secondary, and law enforcement was abandoned as FBI efforts focused on containing "subversives" by extralegal methods.

During the World War II period the FBI won positive acclaim for its apprehension of Nazi agents and sympathizers seeking to subvert the nation's military effort and defense production. The most notable of these involved the arrest in 1942 of eight German saboteurs before their attempt to commit sabotage, and the seizure in 1940 of members of the German American Bund on charges of attempting to relay defense information to Germany.

Still, between 1936 and 1945 the apprehension and prosecution of German agents and sympathizers engaged in sabotage and espionage constituted only a fraction of FBI activities. Increasingly after 1936 FBI efforts shifted from law enforcement (including prosecution of spies and saboteurs) to the collection of "intelligence."* The principal target of FBI investigations—even after the United States became a military ally of the Soviet Union against the fascist powers of Germany, Italy, and Japan—became American Communists and left-wing trade unionists and political activists.

*Hoover distinguished between "intelligence" and "investigative" activity. Investigative activity, the FBI director maintained, "is conducted when there is a specific violation of a Criminal Statute involved, always presupposes an overt act and is proceeded upon with the very definite intention of developing facts and information that will enable prosecution under such legislation." In contrast, intelligence activity "is predicated upon an entirely different premise." That premise, Hoover claimed, was that "Much of the activity indulged in by the Communists and subversive elements does not, in the original stage, involve an overt act or violation of a specific statute. These subversive groups direct their attention to the dissemination of propaganda and to the boring from within processes, much of which is not a violation of a Federal Statute at the time it is indulged in, but which may become a very definite violation of the law in the event of a declaration of war or of the declaration of a national emergency."

During a secret meeting with President Roosevelt in August 1936, Hoover described in detail fascist and Communist political activities in the United States, emphasizing in particular Communist influence in the International Longshoremen, United Mine Workers, and Newspaper Guild unions. "The Communists," Hoover warned, "had planned to get control of these three [unions] and by doing so they would be able to paralyze the country." The president responded by requesting "a survey" of these "conditions" and asked that this "be handled quite confidentially."

Roosevelt's request, and his insistence on confidentiality, provided the opening which the ambitious FBI director quickly exploited to focus FBI investigations on "subversive activities." Then, after the outbreak of the European war with the German invasion of Poland in September 1939 and President Roosevelt's efforts to develop support for a more interventionist foreign policy, Hoover unhesitatingly abetted Roosevelt's efforts to challenge the loyalty of his isolationist critics in Congress and among the general public. Whether he was responding to specific White House requests or volunteering information on the "subversive activities" of the administration's foreign policy critics (on both the left and right), Hoover turned the FBI into the intelligence arm of the White House.

The FBI director did not, for the most part, report evidence of espionage or sabotage. Instead he advised the White House of the plans and tactics of isolationists who opposed FDR's drive to amend the neutrality laws or authorize Lend-Lease. The FBI also closely monitored the reporting of the right-wing isolationist press, notably the *Chicago Tribune,* the *Washington Times-Herald,* and the *New York Daily News,* and maintained surveillance on *Times-Herald* publisher Eleanor Patterson, *Daily News* publisher J. M. Patterson, and *Tribune* reporters Chesly Manly and Stanley Johnston. Pressured by President Roosevelt after Pearl Harbor to take action "against publishers of seditious matter," Hoover lamented that "his hands were tied" by Attorney General Francis Biddle. Biddle's insistence on evidence of illegal conduct effectively rebuffed FBI efforts to prosecute the president's right-wing press critics.

An undaunted Hoover also sought to ingratiate himself with a sympathetic president by providing detailed reports on the plans and thoughts of German, Italian, Vichy French, and Soviet embassy officials, based on electronic surveillance of their embassies in Washington. Despite the wartime military alliance between the United States and the Soviet Union, the FBI continued after 1941 intensively to monitor American Communist party leaders, acquiring information through illegal wiretaps, bugs, break-ins, mail opening, and the interception of international messages. Hoover's regular reports to the White House offered no evidence of Communist espionage on behalf of the Soviet Union but instead recounted the source and dollar amount of Soviet funding of the U.S. Communist party and party officials' reactions to the president's foreign policy decisions, policies regarding strikes and labor disputes, and efforts to preclude the deportation of International Longshoremen union president Harry Bridges or the prosecution of Communist party leader

Earl Browder on passport fraud. Indeed, Hoover's reports to the president on the internal security situation confirmed his obsession with left-wing political activities. For example, a 131-page report of August 1944, captioned "General Intelligence Survey in the United States," devoted 33 pages to German, Japanese, and Italian activities and 62 pages to Communist, "Communist Front," and "Communist Activities in Organized Labor."

This shift in the FBI's role after 1936 was not publicly known. Intelligence about dissident political activities was quietly disseminated to the White House, the State, Justice, and Treasury departments, and the military intelligence agencies. It may not have benefited the war effort, but it did alert senior federal officials to the political plans and strategies of right-wing and left-wing political activists. Because the FBI had obtained much of this information illegally, even the evidence of Soviet funding could not be used to prosecute the American Communist party leadership under the Foreign Agent Registration Act of 1940. But if Hoover was unable to exploit the FBI's discoveries about Communists and their left-liberal allies during the war years, the accumulated information acquired greater value after 1945 in the changed political climate of the cold war.

Convinced that American radicals—and not only Communist party members—threatened the nation's security, Hoover was no longer content to share information only with senior administration officials. In February 1946 he launched an "educational campaign" to "influence public opinion." Intended to educate the public to the threat posed by the Communist party and "by the support that the Party receives from 'Liberal' sources and from its connections in the labor unions," this covert program relied upon carefully prepared "educational material which can be released through available channels so that in the event of an emergency we will have an informed public opinion."

Hoover inaugurated this educational campaign without the knowledge and authorization of the Truman White House. If it was avowedly anti-Communist, it succeeded because FBI officials could exploit the anti–New Deal objectives of the administration's conservative adversaries in Congress and the media. Begun cautiously and ad hoc in 1946, the campaign soon expanded in scope and purpose. It embraced covert, informal assistance to the House Committee on Un-American Activities (notably during its highly publicized hearings of 1947–1948 into Communist influence in Hollywood and in the wake of Whittaker Chambers's charges against Alger Hiss); carefully orchestrated assistance and advice to Senator Joseph McCarthy dating from March 1950; a formal liaison program with the Senate Internal Security Subcommittee from February 1951; a code-named Responsibilities Program also begun in 1951, under which information was leaked to governors and state officials; and carefully controlled leaks to favored reporters, columnists, and editors (notably Walter Trohan, Lyle Wilson, Frederick Woltman, Don Whitehead, George Sokolsky, Fulton Lewis, Jr., Walter Winchell, Newbold Noyes, and David Lawrence). The culmination of these separate but interrelated activities was the inception of a formal Mass Media program and the now infamous COINTELPROs in the 1950s. With the COINTELPROs, FBI officials moved beyond dissemination to aggressively "harass, disrupt, or discredit" targeted radical organizations—the Communist party, the Socialist Workers party, white supremacist organizations such as the Ku Klux Klan, black nationalist organizations such as the Black Panthers, and the New Left.

The FBI's various dissemination activities marked a decided shift from law enforcement to political containment. The underlying objective of shaping public opinion also informed the FBI's publicized efforts to safeguard the nation's internal security, whether by purging suspected radicals from the federal bureaucracy (through the presidentially authorized Federal Employee Loyalty Program) or by prosecuting Communist party leaders under the Smith Act or the accused spies Alger Hiss, William Remington, and Julius and Ethel Rosenberg. Publicizing these examples of Communist infiltration and espionage also helped alert the public to the seriousness of the Red Menace.

In the process, Hoover circumvented the constitutional limitations on FBI investigative practices. When he demanded and gained confidentiality for FBI sources in the administration of the loyalty program, Hoover succeeded in laundering illegally obtained information that was used to effect the dismissal of radical and Popular Front liberals from the federal bureaucracy.* Federal loyalty review board

*Information challenging a federal employee's loyalty was reported as having been obtained from a "confidential informant of known reliability," masking whether it came from an informer, a wiretap, or a membership list obtained through a break-in.

hearings did not conform to the rules of evidence of judicial proceedings, so that defendants could not directly challenge the credibility of their accusers or question whether evidence had been illegally obtained.

Interestingly, the FBI did not secure the indictment of Communist party leaders for espionage but for violating the vague standards of the so-called Smith Act—participation in a conspiracy to overthrow the United States government by force or violence. To effect prosecution, the FBI did not introduce its most damning evidence of the American Communist party's subservience to the Soviet Union, including receipt of funds, because such information had been illegally obtained through wiretaps, bugs, and break-ins. Instead the Bureau produced informers who offered uncorroborated testimony about the plans and purposes of their coconspirators. Meanwhile, FBI briefs were based on a tendentious analysis of Communist publications, including Marxist-Leninist classics. Ideological evidence and suspect associations were sufficient to ensure convictions in the climate of suspicion and fear produced by the cold war.

The Hiss, Remington, and Rosenberg cases offer further insights into Hoover's politics of crime. Although these cases were popularly understood as illustrations of Soviet espionage, they were not developed through FBI counterintelligence operations. Only the Rosenbergs were indicted on espionage charges. Hiss's and Remington's indictments were for perjury—they denied giving classified documents to known Communist couriers. The FBI did not prove in court that Hiss, Remington, and the Rosenbergs committed espionage. The Rosenberg and Remington convictions were based on the uncorroborated testimony of claimed coconspirators while Hiss's accuser alone produced documentation to support his charges.

These cases, even though they were successfully prosecuted, should have raised questions about the FBI's counterintelligence abilities. Hiss was tried in 1949 for alleged espionage conducted in 1938; the Rosenbergs and Remington were tried in 1950 for alleged activities during World War II. Yet the FBI suffered little criticism for failing to have prevented espionage. Instead, the political objectives of America's cold war conservatives made these cases a public relations bonanza for Hoover.

Rather than question the FBI's competence, conservatives in the media and in Congress portrayed these cases as confirming the Roosevelt and Truman administrations' "softness toward Communism." Rallying to the defense of Hoover and the FBI, conservatives denounced the Democrats for ignoring FBI reports that might have permitted an earlier discovery of Communist espionage.

The anti-Communist obsession of the cold war years caused presidents, members of Congress, and the media to overlook Hoover's definition of the "subversive" threat. This reduced accountability invited the FBI director to expand the Bureau's investigations beyond Communist party members and radical revolutionaries to prominent liberals— notably Martin Luther King, Jr., Adlai Stevenson, Henry Wallace, Paul Douglas, Walter Reuther, Arthur Schlesinger, Jr., Chester Bowles, Eleanor Roosevelt, and Senators/Representatives George McGovern, Wayne Morse, George Norris, Claude Pepper, James Roosevelt, Don Edwards, and J. William Fulbright. In addition, "writers, lecturers, newsmen, entertainers, and others in the mass media field" were to be closely monitored owing to their being "in a position to influence others against the national interest."* As an example of such a dangerous influence, Hoover specifically cited "such individuals as Norman Mailer, a novelist and author of *The Naked and the Dead* and an admitted 'leftist.'"

This politics of crime did not come without cost to the FBI's law enforcement responsibilities. Hoover's demand that FBI agents investigate and contain "subversive" activists required a vast expenditure of manpower. Eight to ten agents were normally required to conduct a break-in while bugs and wiretaps required round-the-clock attention and then transcription of the intercepted conversations. Officials at FBI headquarters devoted long hours to supervising COINTELPRO proposals, implementing the Sex Deviates and Responsibilities programs, and processing name-check requests or volunteering information to the White House and favored congressional committees, members of Congress, reporters, and columnists. Even though the number of FBI agents increased from approximately nine hundred in 1940 to ten thousand by the time of Hoover's death in 1972, that increase kept pace with the FBI's intensive monitoring of

*These included the composer Leonard Bernstein, folk singer Pete Seeger, actor Charlie Chaplin, writers Ernest Hemingway and Dwight Macdonald, and reporters Peter Lisagor and Peter Arnett.

"subversive activities." Without further increasing FBI personnel, Hoover's FBI lacked the manpower to launch the labor-intensive and long-term investigations essential to a successful war on organized crime—or to address the equally serious problems of white-collar crime and influence peddling that surfaced as major national crime issues after World War II.

But limited resources alone do not explain the FBI's unimpressive anticrime record. A far more important factor was Hoover's politics of crime, best understood by comparing FBI practices in the two areas of subversive and criminal activities.

Empowered by the Federal Employee Loyalty Program and the Smith Act to monitor radical activities, FBI officials could make use of any noncriminal political and personal information they acquired. Conservatives in the media and the Congress welcomed such information when it was leaked. And prosecution of Communist party officials or radical activists did not require proof of specific acts violating federal laws, only their ideological affinity and suspect associations. In effect, the Smith Act (as interpreted by the Vinson but not the Warren Court) criminalized advocacy and attempts to organize to effect revolutionary change, and the loyalty program's standard of "reasonable doubt" permitted dismissal based on suspect political associations. No such programs or laws existed to combat organized crime until Congress enacted the Federal Racketeering Influence Corrupt Organization Act, or RICO, in

1970).* Prosecution of crime syndicate leaders was Hoover's only option, and it required proof of the commission of specific criminal acts—whether nonpayment of income taxes, the capture of union locals, interstate gambling, or extortion.

*Nor had Hoover thwarted the enactment of legislation to permit the easier prosecution of criminals. RICO was enacted in 1970 because of the widespread concern about "law and order" that had been building since the mid-1960s. Conservatives championed the need to expand federal law enforcement powers, as illustrated by Richard Nixon's and George Wallace's exploitation in the 1968 presidential campaign of the backlash against urban racial disorders and anti–Vietnam War demonstrations. As head of the investigative division of the Department of Justice, Hoover had no authority to draft legislation and then lobby Congress for its passage—that was the responsibility of the attorney general and senior department officials who were unable until the 1960s to undercut Congress's reluctance to expand federal enforcement powers. This limited influence was particularly underscored by the department's failure, even in the McCarthy era, to legalize wiretapping and modify preventive detention standards. Dating from 1941, every president (from Franklin Roosevelt through John Kennedy) and their attorneys general unsuccessfully lobbied Congress to rescind the 1934 Federal Communications Act's ban on wiretapping. Only in 1968 was such legislation enacted.

Although Hoover unilaterally established a preventive detention program in 1939, continued a Custodial Detention program under a different name after 1943 when Attorney General Biddle banned it, and then in 1948 obtained Attorney General Tom Clark's approval for a Security Index program, the preventive detention legislation passed by Congress in 1950 (not knowing of Hoover's secret program) was far more protective of individual liberties. In response, FBI and Justice Department officials decided to ignore the legislatively mandated standards and unsuccessfully lobbied Congress to amend the 1950 McCarran Act to conform to their ongoing Security Index program. Not only did this legislative effort fail, but when Congress in 1971 repealed the McCarran Act's preventive detention title, Hoover convinced Attorney General John Mitchell to continue his secret program, now renamed Administrative Index.

138

Despite Hoover's depiction of a sinister, omnipresent Communist conspiracy, the FBI had in fact massively infiltrated the Communist party and other radical organizations—and was able to rely on the uncorroborated testimony of its National Defense Informants during the various internal security proceedings of the cold war era. FBI officials similarly attempted to develop Criminal Informants to infiltrate the Mafia but were generally unsuccessful. Informing on the Mob was risky and not as remunerative as remaining a loyal Mafioso.

That Hoover until the late 1950s publicly denied the existence of a nationwide criminal conspiracy was not due to disinterest or a lack of the same anecdotal evidence about Mafia connections and activities that was publicized by crime reporters and criminologists. Rather, Hoover's FBI could not meet its law enforcement responsibilities in the area of organized crime—unless the FBI director, at minimum, sacrificed the politically effective pursuit of subversives. He would have had to shift resources to investigate crime syndicates and, just as important, devise lawful methods to acquire evidence that could withstand the adversary proceedings of a criminal trial.

So Hoover played down the importance of organized crime. But his hand was called in 1957. On November 14 New York state trooper Edgar Croswell observed the arrival of a stream of limousines with out-of-state license plates at the secluded estate of Joseph Barbara in Apalachin, New York. Establishing a roadblock ostensibly to determine if the drivers had valid identification required under New

York motor vehicle laws, Croswell eventually identified sixty-three of Barbara's guests, all of whom claimed to be businessmen and were of Italian descent, among them Vito Genovese, Joseph Bonanno, Joseph Profaci, Carmine Galante, Thomas Lucchesi, John Scalisi, Stefano Magaddino, and Santos Trafficante—all known organized-crime bosses. This apparent confirmation of the Mafia's existence proved to be a public relations disaster for Hoover. Within days after the Apalachin story broke, the FBI director initiated a code-named Top Hoodlum program. SACs of all FBI field offices were ordered to identify the "top hoodlums" in their geographic area and to prepare detailed reports on the activities of known organized-crime leaders.

Establishing a formal Top Hoodlum program did little to resolve what had historically undermined the FBI's war on crime—the inability to develop legally admissible evidence of federal law violations. Unable to recruit informers, and reluctant to have FBI agents infiltrate crime syndicates, Hoover decided to employ the techniques that had proven successful in the FBI's war on "subversives"—wiretaps, break-ins, and bugs. But in the case of organized crime, this decision had quite different consequences. It determined why the FBI failed to neutralize the Mafia and why Hoover never fully briefed the various attorneys general on the information the FBI acquired.

When it enacted the Federal Communications Act in 1934, Congress banned wiretapping. Then, in 1937, the Supreme Court ruled that this legislative ban applied to federal agents, and in 1939 that any resort to wiretapping during a criminal investigation tainted and required the dismissal of the case. Despite this legislative ban and the Court's rulings, in May 1940 President Roosevelt secretly authorized FBI wiretapping during "national defense" investigations. President Truman extended FBI wiretapping authority in July 1946 to include "cases vitally affecting the domestic security or where human life is in jeopardy."

Roosevelt's secret directive did not legalize FBI wiretapping—even though he had privately concluded that the Court's ruling was limited to criminal cases, not to actions designed to prevent espionage or sabotage. Nonetheless, to minimize the discovery of this practice and to ensure that FBI wiretapping met his "national defense" standard, FDR required the attorney general's prior approval in each case. This oversight role was strengthened in 1952 in the aftermath of the Judith Coplon case.*

An FBI wiretap, then, in effect immunized a targeted crime leader from prosecution. And because he was required to obtain the attorney general's advance approval to wiretap

---

*An employee of the Justice Department's alien registration section, Coplon was indicted in 1949 for unauthorized possession of classified FBI documents with the intention of delivering them to an agent of a foreign power (a Soviet employee on the United Nations staff). During her trial it was disclosed that the FBI had tapped Coplon's phone before and after her arrest. This disclosure had embarrassing consequences because Justice Department attorneys had not known of the wiretapping before trial, and because the belated admission of wiretapping subverted Coplon's conviction. To ensure that the department was not blindsided again, Attorney General J. Howard McGrath directed Hoover to notify the Justice Department whenever the FBI had wiretapped during an investigation and before the department's presentation of the case to a grand jury for indictment.

a crime syndicate boss, Hoover thereby tacitly signaled his willingness to forgo prosecution.

For Hoover, break-ins, in contrast, posed quite different problems and opportunities. When Hoover decided in 1942 to use this technique regularly, the FBI director nonetheless conceded that break-ins were "clearly illegal." Thus he never sought to "obtain legal sanction" (i.e., the prior approval of the attorney general) but instead devised a sophisticated system to minimize the risk of discovery of this illegal activity. SACs were required to obtain his (or a designated FBI assistant director's) prior approval and "completely justify the need for the use of the technique and at the same time assure that it can be safely used without any danger or embarrassment to the Bureau." Written requests for such authorization were to be captioned "Do Not File," ensuring that these communications were not indexed and filed in the FBI's official records system. Instead they were routed to nonrecorded office files. This procedure permitted the undiscoverable destruction of all break-in records and allowed FBI officials to respond, whether to court-ordered discovery motions or congressional subpoenas, that a search of the FBI's "central records system" had uncovered no evidence of illegal activity.

Great care was also taken in effecting the break-in. Agents first surveyed the targeted office, home, or apartment to identify any security systems and to learn the normal activity patterns of the occupant and neighbors. On the day of the break-in, one or two agents would tail the occupant (maintaining contact by walkie-talkie with the supervisor of the break-in squad in the event the subject suddenly returned to the break-in site); three to four agents would monitor the outside of the building or hallway while two agents entered the premises, one to retrieve and the other to photocopy documents or install a bug.*

Break-ins permitted the FBI to acquire "highly secret and closely guarded material," such as financial records, correspondence, and subscription or membership lists. Owing to the confidentiality of these records, FBI officials could not report these discoveries outside the Bureau unless they somehow laundered the information to meet standards of legal admissibility. In most Top Hoodlum investigations, the FBI was unable to recruit informers and could not meet the probable-cause standard to obtain a warrant to search the premises. Thus FBI officials could not turn this intelligence into legally admissible evidence to indict and convict organized-crime leaders—or even brief the attorney general on the resulting discoveries.

As examples: In December 1957 FBI agents broke into the apartment of a New York City crime boss to photocopy his papers, correspondence, and photographs (the latter to identify other crime associates). Unable to break into the residence or meeting place of another crime leader, and on

---

*FBI agents have recounted how they responded to unanticipated crises during break-ins. In one case, when an agent slipped off a joist in the attic of a mob hangout in Chicago, he and his colleagues successfully plastered the hole he had caused. When surprised by the sudden appearance of a police officer or the occupant, agents knocked out the unwelcome intruder and ransacked the residence to make it appear that a robbery had been interrupted.

the understanding that he spent "considerable time with his girl friend," in May and then again in October 1958 FBI agents broke into her apartment and photocopied notes, letters, other documents, and photographs. Upon learning that a Top Hoodlum in Newark, New Jersey, frequently used his attorney's office to conduct business and to meet with various criminal associates, in December 1963 FBI agents broke into the attorney's office to photocopy business records and correspondence—claiming there was "no known attorney-client relationship" between the Newark crime boss and this attorney.

While in these cases the acquired information could not be laundered, in other cases such illegally obtained information was helpful in developing leads and then in acquiring lawfully admissible evidence. In January 1964 agents broke into the apartment of an individual under investigation in a White Slave Traffic Act case; in March 1959 agents broke into the apartment of a suspect under investigation for stealing $400,000 in jewelry from the Americana Hotel in Bal Harbour, Florida; in December 1961 agents broke into the office of "allegedly the largest shylocking operation in the US"; in June 1962 agents broke into a Yonkers office used for recording horse bets during an interstate gambling investigation; and in April 1962 agents broke into the office of a New York union local under investigation for suspected criminal influence to photocopy receipts, business cards, personal material, and a telephone address book. We have these examples only because the New York SAC unaccountably failed to destroy break-in records—thus contravening Bureau policy—from 1954 to 1973.

In contrast to wiretaps, break-ins were not known to the attorney general. Thus in certain cases they could be helpful in promoting prosecution. While microphone surveillance (bugging) also required an illegal entry to install the bug, this practice posed distinctive problems owing to the role of the attorney general.

When he formally established the Do Not File procedure in 1942, Hoover authorized break-ins both to photocopy documents and to install bugs. In contrast to wiretaps, until October 1951 FBI bugging installations were done without the prior knowledge and authorization of the attorney general. That year, responding to the policy problems posed by the Judith Coplon case, Hoover for the first time briefed the attorney general on FBI bugging practices. Responding to Hoover's briefing on February 26, 1952, Attorney General J. Howard McGrath said he had no problems with the "use of microphone surveillance which does not involve a trespass" (that is, spike microphones, installed in the wall of an adjoining office or apartment). But when bugs were installed through trespass, McGrath added, this fell "in the area of the Fourth Amendment, and evidence so obtained and from leads so obtained is inadmissible," and as such "I cannot authorize the installation of a microphone *involving a trespass* under existing law."

McGrath did not order Hoover to *stop* this practice. Not surprisingly, the FBI continued to break in to install microphones. McGrath's written conclusion that such installations were illegal caused Hoover some concern, but this was alleviated with the election of the more sympathetic Republican administration of Dwight Eisenhower in 1952.

Citing the Supreme Court's recent decision in *Irvine v. California* (where the Court had overturned a conviction based on the California state police's installation of a microphone in a bedroom during a criminal investigation), in 1954 Hoover wrote Attorney General Herbert Brownell of the FBI's need for "some backing of the [Justice] Department to utilize microphone surveillance where the intelligence to be gained was a necessary adjunct to security matters and important investigations, in instances where prosecution is not contemplated." To provide this backing, Hoover recommended that Brownell adopt the same procedure governing wiretaps—prior review and authorization by the attorney general for each use.

Although he favored such uses during "national security" investigations, Brownell was unwilling to accept the proposed oversight responsibilities inherent in Hoover's recommendation. Instead, on May 20 he issued a broadly worded, secret directive giving Hoover blanket authority to install bugs, including by trespass, as the "only possible way of uncovering the activities of espionage agents, possible saboteurs, and subversive persons." The attorney general agreed to adopt the broadest interpretation of the Fourth Amendment "which will permit microphone coverage by the FBI in a manner more conducive to the national interest. I recognize that for the FBI to fulfill its important intelligence functions, considerations of internal security and the national safety are paramount and, therefore, may compel the unrestricted use of this technique in the national interest."

Brownell's refusal to oversee each FBI bugging operation invited Hoover to employ this technique extensively, in most cases without ever notifying or seeking the ex post facto approval of the attorney general. Unwilling to confine such uses to national security investigations, on May 21 (the day after Brownell's secret approval) Hoover and senior FBI officials unilaterally interpreted his directive as authorizing FBI bugging not only during "coverage such as Communist Party underground and Soviet Intelligence matters" but also in "important" criminal cases—though in these instances such installations would "only be approved by high Bureau officials." The FBI only sporadically installed bugs during criminal investigations until Hoover established the Top Hoodlum program in 1957. Seeking ways to extend the FBI's ability to obtain information about organized crime leaders in the wake of the Apalachin embarrassment, in July 1959 Hoover again unilaterally decided to expand the FBI's uses of bugs.

FBI Assistant Director Alan Belmont rationalized this decision. The purpose of the Top Hoodlum program, Belmont argued, was as "an intelligence effort" (not prosecutive) "directed against top criminal leaders and organized crime," and the Bureau's need to "develop intelligence in this area" justified using "microphones against top hoodlums on the basis of the threat to society from organized crime." Brownell's secret 1954 directive had been "primarily directed toward security matters," Belmont acknowledged, but its "terminology 'national safety' was interpreted by the Bureau to include criminal cases."

Belmont's assessment was formally reviewed by Hoover and senior FBI officials, who debated whether to seek Attorney General William Rogers's (Brownell's successor) "approval" before authorizing an expanded use of bugs during criminal investigations. This need not be done, Hoover eventually concluded, as the FBI was "adequately protected" by the language of Brownell's 1954 directive covering "both Security and Criminal matters."

Hoover's unilateral and effectively insubordinate decision nonetheless posed two quite different problems. Brownell's directive did not legalize such installations, and had been issued on the understanding that such uses would be confined to counterintelligence operations. Having decided unilaterally to bug organized-crime leaders, Hoover could neither advise the attorney general that bugs had been installed during Top Hoodlum investigations nor report the intelligence that had been acquired.

Hoover's decision in effect compromised the Justice Department's abilities to prosecute organized-crime leaders—and by 1966 complicated an already tense relationship with Attorney General Nicholas Katzenbach.* Addressing

*In March 1965 Katzenbach instituted new rules governing FBI microphone surveillances: advance approval by the attorney general for each installation, but only for six months, requiring Hoover to seek reauthorization every six months. Katzenbach's rules forced Hoover in 1965 to seek the attorney general's after-the-fact authorization for 35 antiracketeering bugs that the FBI had unilaterally installed between 1962 and

Hoover's query whether the FBI should inform Katzenbach "concerning the extent" of the FBI's bugging practices in light of the attorney general's 1965 rules and the problems posed by the Fred Black case (discussed later in this chapter), FBI Assistant Director James Gale pointed out that of the 738 bugs installed between 1960 and 1966, FBI officials had informed senior Justice Department officials of only 158 of these installations. (Gale did not spell out the criteria used to decide when FBI officials did or did not notify the department.) The FBI should not, Gale continued, inform senior Justice Department officials of FBI bugging practices as this "could result only in the Department running to the courts with the resultant adverse publicity to the Bureau which could give rise in the present climate to a demand for a Congressional inquiry of the Bureau." Only when prosecution was "imminent" should Justice Department officials be notified. Yet even in these cases, Gale added, such notification might adversely affect prosecution:

> To make available to the Department, voluntarily, the extent of our use of this technique, could well serve as a further deterrent to an aggressive attitude looking toward prosecution. In numerous of our top hoodlum cases, the Department has frequently found

---

1964. Later that year Hoover also sought Katzenbach's prior approval for an additional 9 bugs. Even so, Hoover did not provide notice and seek authorization for all FBI bugs of "top hoodlums." Of the 380 such bugs installed between 1960 and 1966, only 64 "were known to the [Justice] Department."

legal reasons or confidential reasons as justification for their failure to initiate prosecution.

In remarks underscoring the culture of lawlessness which defined FBI investigative activities and priorities, Gale pointed out:

> The Department has successfully prosecuted 15 hoodlums of whom we are aware, but of whom the Department had no knowledge of our microphone coverage. It is seriously questioned whether the Department would have pursued these prosecutions if they had known of the existence of our coverage, even though no evidence utilized during the course of the trial was of a tainted nature. To elect to advise the Department at this time would probably result in the Department's decision to petition the courts for reopening the matter.

Gale's stark admission that the FBI did not (and should not) inform Justice Department officials of its illegal bugging practices, and his underlying disdain for the constitutional concerns of Justice Department officials, help explain why Hoover neither briefed senior Justice Department officials of the intelligence gained from bugs nor met departmental demands to develop cases against organized-crime leaders.

Gale's attitude was the norm among senior FBI officials. When a New York agent attending an FBI training class in Washington in 1955 remarked that he thought break-ins were unconstitutional, FBI officials investigated the New York office to determine whether "his mental outlook might be present" among those agents who comprised that office's break-in squad—and if it was, to "determine which of these men should be retained on this type of activity and which should be deleted." The inquiry found that this agent had had no contact with members of the break-in squad, and that none of the squad members shared his scruples about constitutionality.

Hoover's own attitudes about the law are more graphically captured in one of his responses to the crisis of his authority and public reputation posed by the Fred Black case.

A Washington-based lobbyist named Fred Black became the target of an FBI investigation in 1962 because of his gambling associations and influence peddling. In the course of this investigation, in December 1962 Hoover unilaterally authorized the bugging of Black's office and residence. FBI officials did not advise Justice Department officials of this practice when the department in 1963 secured an indictment of Black for income tax evasion. Only later in August 1965, in the course of briefing department officials on their bugging of Teamsters president Jimmy Hoffa, did FBI officials disclose the earlier bugging of Black. As a result, when the Black case came before the Supreme Court on appeal in 1966, Attorney General Nicholas Katzenbach directed Solicitor General Thurgood Marshall to inform the Court of this bug. The Court thereupon demanded that the government submit a brief outlining the legal authority for this installation. Having learned that none of his immediate predecessors as attorney general (Brownell, Rogers, and Robert Kennedy) were aware of FBI bugging during criminal investigations (all claimed knowledge only of such uses during "national security" investigations), Katzenbach's proposed brief reported that FBI bugs had been installed without explicit departmental authorization. Hoover was infuriated with the language of this brief, which he believed would tarnish the Bureau's and his own reputation. He pressed Katzenbach to revise it, but he was unsuccessful. The FBI director then appealed to the anti-Kennedy biases of Rogers, President Johnson, and Senator Edward Long by suggesting that Katzenbach was purposefully protecting Robert Kennedy (during whose attorney generalship the bug was installed and the indictment of Black obtained).

As part of this end run to question Katzenbach's political loyalties, FBI Assistant Director Cartha DeLoach secretly contacted Supreme Court justice Abe Fortas. Knowing of Fortas's partisan relationship with President Johnson, De-Loach succeeded because the Supreme Court justice accepted DeLoach's account of this matter as "a continuing fight for the Presidency" between Robert Kennedy and Johnson. And despite the fact that this case was then before the Supreme Court, Fortas shared the Court's private deliberations with two interested parties, the FBI and the Johnson White House, and then proposed a method to promote both Hoover's objective and Johnson's political interests.[*]

*Fortas's proposal was that President Johnson appoint a three-member commission to mediate this dispute—with the membership agreeable to the president and to Hoover. Johnson at first acceded but soon decided

DeLoach immediately briefed Hoover on his meeting with Fortas. Conceding that DeLoach's initiative had apparently succeeded, Hoover admitted to having been

> dubious as I didn't know Fortas well myself, but I thought he would try to weasel out on grounds it was improper for him as a member of the Court to even discuss the matter and then, of course, nothing could have been obtained, but he apparently is a more honest man than I gave him credit for. DeLoach stated that it boils down to the fact that he has to defend the President.

Hoover's comment not only sheds light on his conception of government officials' ethical responsibilities but succinctly captures the essence of the FBI's failure as a law enforcement agency. From 1936 Hoover for the most part abandoned law enforcement, preferring instead a politics of crime based on the imperative need to monitor and contain "subversive activities." To achieve this, the FBI director willingly authorized illegal investigative techniques and used the acquired information to discredit radical activists through federal loyalty proceedings or the willing collaboration of conservatives in Congress and the media. Emboldened by this success and embarrassed by the Apalachin revelations,

---

against this course of action, recognizing that this implicit questioning of Katzenbach's authority would publicize the conflict and lead Katzenbach to resign. Instead, a suspicious Johnson eased Katzenbach out of the attorney generalship.

Hoover later decided to repair the FBI's inability to infiltrate organized-crime syndicates by using illegal investigative techniques. But in this case a politics of crime could not cripple criminal leaders who cared little about their public reputation. Their power could be contained only through prosecution and conviction. Yet because the most revealing information had been illegally obtained by the FBI, prosecution was hindered. Nor could the acquired intelligence be shared with Hoover's superiors in the Justice Department. A lawless agency, and an insubordinate FBI director, proved incapable of functioning as an effective law enforcement agency.

CONCLUSION

Hoover,
the Law,
and Politics

IT was only after Hoover's death in 1972 that investigating organized crime became an FBI priority, the ironic byproduct of his abuses of power. It came about beginning in 1975, when Congress initiated its first intensive inquiry into the practices of the federal intelligence agencies, and the focus turned on the FBI and the CIA. The catalysts to this congressional interest were revelations first of President Nixon's political uses of the agencies and then of FBI and CIA programs violating privacy and First Amendment rights—notably that Hoover had maintained a secret office file containing derogatory information on prominent Americans. Congressional hearings and reports of 1975–1976 publicized the scope and illegality of Hoover's monitoring and harassment of political activists.

Forced on the defensive, and to restore public confidence, FBI Directors Clarence Kelley, William Webster, and William Sessions publicly scaled back FBI "domestic security" investigations and announced that the Bureau would concentrate on organized and white-collar crime. With new strategies (such as the use of profiling, undercover agents, lasers, computers, video cameras, and DNA testing) and relaxed dress codes, FBI officials abandoned the rigidity of Hoover's administrative style. These efforts eventually bore fruit in the 1980s with a series of indictments and convictions of notorious crime syndicate leaders in New York, Milwaukee, Tampa, and Kansas City.

Even had Hoover remained FBI director after 1972, the FBI's organized crime record would have improved. The reason is that legislation enacted at the end of his tenure—RICO in 1970 and, more important, the Omnibus Crime Control and Safe Streets Act in 1968—made it easier to prosecute organized-crime bosses. Significantly, the principal evidence leading to the FBI's victories in the 1980s resulted from the legalization of wiretapping and bugging in 1968.

Although the practice had been prohibited by law before 1968, Hoover's FBI had wiretapped and bugged political activists and crime bosses—including Meyer Lansky, Sam Giancana, John Roselli, Frank Balistrieri, Phil Alderisio, Willie Alderman, and Carlos Marcello. But the FBI could not use the information it acquired. Nor could Hoover publicize these FBI actions or rebut the rare criticisms voiced during the 1960s of the FBI's crime-fighting efforts. To do so would only have highlighted his disdain for the law and his duplicity while he professed the FBI's respect for the limitations of its lawful authority.

In addition to his ineffectiveness against organized crime, Hoover's secretiveness and independence created a culture of lawlessness within the ranks of the FBI.* FBI agents

*FBI Assistant Director William Sullivan's 1975 interview with the Special Senate Committee on Intelligence Activities captures this mind-

should have known that they were violating the Fourth Amendment when they broke in to install bugs or to photocopy documents, and that they were acting outside the law when they disseminated information under the Mass Media program or devised proposals to "harass, disrupt or discredit" radical activists. In rewarding agents for these activities, Hoover created an action-oriented agency whose personnel shared his conviction of the righteousness of their objectives.

When monitoring political activists and crime bosses, FBI personnel understood the political imperatives that made it necessary to conceal their extralegal actions. Steeled to flaunt the law, over time they came to resent even Hoover's strict rules and cautions to preclude public discovery, leading some to secret insubordination. Thus FBI agents ignored Hoover's requirement of advance approval for break-ins; they broke in first and then requested his authorization. Some SACs, notably Neil Welch,* secretly conducted investigations which did not follow Hoover's guidelines and priorities. This insubordination reached its apogee in 1970

---

set. "Never once," Sullivan admitted, did he or any other member of the U.S. Intelligence Board "raise the question: 'Is this course of action which we have agreed upon lawful, is it legal, is it ethical or moral?' We never gave any thought to this realm of questioning, because we were just naturally pragmatists. The one thing we were concerned about was this: will this course of action work, will it get us what we want, will we reach the objective that we desire to reach."

*Welch served as SAC in Buffalo, Detroit, and Philadelphia and articulated the disdain that many agents in the field felt toward Hoover and his senior aides. The best way to improve law enforcement, he remarked, would be to "sandbag Bureau headquarters and rip out the phones."

when FBI Assistant Director William Sullivan went behind
Hoover's back and secretly collaborated with Nixon White
House aide Tom Charles Huston in an attempt to cir-
cumvent the FBI director's recently imposed restrictions on
the FBI's uses of "clearly illegal" investigative techniques.

This counterreality never surfaced during Hoover's tenure
as FBI director, nor did the FBI's deficient crime-fighting
efforts ever become a political issue. But this was not
because Hoover's possession of damning personal information helped him to blackmail presidents, attorneys
general, members of Congress, and reporters into silence. In
effect they blackmailed themselves, acquiescing in Hoover's
abusive directorship of the FBI because they welcomed his
willingness to provide them with information they could
deny receiving.

Although it was atypical in the scope of its abuses of
power, Richard Nixon's presidency provides an unprecedented record of this sort of covert relationship between
presidents and Hoover: through Nixon's taping of conversations in the Oval Office. From these tapes we learn of the
president's intention in October 1971 to demand Hoover's
retirement—and his backing down during the personal
meeting he had arranged with Hoover for this purpose.
Having earlier requested that Hoover conduct illegal investigations (including wiretapping members of his own White
House and National Security Council staffs and prominent
Washington reporters), Nixon decided not to risk Hoover's
displeasure and the possible disclosure of his own misconduct when the FBI director refused gracefully to step

down. This appreciation of Hoover's usefulness is captured in Nixon's February 28, 1973, conversation with White House aide John Dean concerning the enveloping Watergate crisis. Responding to Nixon's characterization of Hoover as "my crony" and as "closer to me than [to President Lyndon] Johnson, although Johnson used him more," Dean remarked that "we would have been a lot better off during this whole Watergate thing if [Hoover] had been alive. Because he knew how to handle that Bureau—knew how to keep things in bounds." Nixon agreed, adding, "Well, Hoover performed. He would have fought. That was the point. He would have defied a few people. He would have scared them to death. He has a file on everybody."

If presidents were unwilling to monitor Hoover's FBI for political reasons, so were their attorneys general. When President Roosevelt secretly authorized FBI wiretapping during "national defense" investigations, but required the prior approval of the attorney general, Robert Jackson (FDR's attorney general) "decided that he would have no detailed record kept concerning the cases in which wire-tapping could be utilized. It was agreeable to him that I [Hoover] would maintain a memorandum book in my immediate office listing the time, places, and cases in which this procedure is to be utilized."

Jackson's refusal to maintain records (a stance continued by his successors) meant that attorneys general could only learn about ongoing FBI wiretaps if they were notified by Hoover, further impairing their ability to judge whether the acquired information met a national defense standard. Nor was this practice confined to wiretapping. When he secretly authorized FBI bugging activities in 1954, Attorney General Herbert Brownell rejected Hoover's proposal to have the attorney general authorize each installation. Brownell's broadly worded directive instead gave Hoover a blank check as to target, purpose, and length of the installed bug. This indifference was abandoned only during the attorney general-ships of Nicholas Katzenbach and Ramsey Clark, when Hoover was required to submit written requests justifying the need for each proposed wiretap and bug, seek their reauthorization every six months, and create a special index listing the names of all individuals whose conversations had been intercepted. Not surprisingly, the number of FBI "national security" wiretaps declined from 519 in 1945, 322 in 1954, and 244 in 1963 to 82 in 1968; the number of bugs fell from 186 in 1945, 102 in 1955, and 100 in 1962 to 0 in 1967 and 9 in 1968.

Hoover's relationship with reporters and members of Congress was even more crassly political, determined by the anti-Communist politics of the cold war era. Indeed, Hoover could not have launched the FBI's successful "educational campaign" in 1946 without the complicity of reporters, editors, and members of Congress who accepted leaked information on the condition that they not disclose the FBI's covert assistance. Rather than monitor the FBI like any other federal agency and evaluate its effectiveness in fighting organized crime, reporters and members of Congress willingly acted to defend Hoover's FBI from criticism and to promote the FBI director's anti-Communist crusade.

For example, in 1949–1950 Hoover was concerned about adverse publicity resulting from revelations of FBI wire-tapping and surveillance activities during Judith Coplon's trial, and then the publication of Max Lowenthal's critical history of the FBI. The FBI director decided to publicize instead the Bureau's professionalism and abiding respect for the law. As part of this public relations strategy, FBI Assistant Director Louis Nichols urged *Reader's Digest* editor Fulton Oursler to publish an article by ACLU attorney Morris Ernst defending the FBI. Oursler agreed but then rejected the submitted article, finding it too pedantic and unin-teresting for the *Digest*'s readers. Nichols convinced Oursler to reconsider his rejection by offering to revise Ernst's leaden prose and liven the narrative with a series of interesting examples. Published in December 1950 and titled "Why I No Longer Fear the FBI," Ernst's article appeared to be an independent assessment by a seemingly critical civil libertarian.

As another example, South Dakota Senator Karl Mundt periodically wrote Hoover to request FBI reports on specified individuals as part of his efforts to highlight the Communist threat. In every case Hoover wrote back rejecting the request and affirming the confidentiality of FBI files. In reality, Hoover's letter of denial was hand-delivered to Mundt by an FBI agent who brought along the requested file and was prepared to answer any questions the senator might have about its contents.

Both Oursler and Mundt wittingly participated in this charade—and in neither case were they rewarded with scoops of a major breaking case that affected the nation's security. Sharing Hoover's political conservatism, they helped promote a political climate immunizing Hoover and the FBI from critical scrutiny.

As an astute bureaucrat, Hoover clearly traded in information to advance his own political agenda and bureaucratic interests and to silence criticism of his leadership of the FBI. The fact that the FBI under Hoover had strayed from law enforcement and from the vigorous prosecution of gangsters, which had first catapulted the FBI into national prominence during the 1930s, never became a political problem for Hoover after 1945. Nor did Hoover's sexuality and interest in the sexual activities of prominent Americans determine his leadership of the FBI or the Bureau's record against organized crime. It was never that simple. Hoover became untouchable, an independent agent, and the FBI's contrasting record in the areas of "subversive" and criminal activities was tolerated, because powerful national leaders shared the FBI director's obsessive anticommunism and yet sought to mask their own complicity and indifference to the law. It was politics that catapulted the ambitious FBI director to the pinnacle of national power and allowed him to define FBI priorities and procedures without concern for his government or the law.

A NOTE ON SOURCES

MUCH has been written about Hoover's FBI. The most comprehensive studies include Athan Theoharis, *Spying on Americans: Political Surveillance from Hoover to the Huston Plan* (Philadelphia, 1978); Frank Donner, *The Age of Surveillance* (New York, 1980); Sanford Ungar, *FBI* (Boston, 1975); Robert Goldstein, *Political Repression in Modern America* (Cambridge, Mass., 1978); John Elliff, *The Reform of FBI Intelligence Operations* (Princeton, 1979); and Kenneth O'Reilly, *"Racial Matters": The FBI's Secret File on Black America, 1960–1972* (New York, 1989). Sigmund Diamond, *Compromised Campus: The Collaboration of the Universities with the Intelligence Community* (New York, 1992), and Robin Winks, *Cloak and Gown: Scholars in the Secret War, 1939–1961* (New York, 1987), chronicle FBI surveillance of college faculty and students. Kenneth O'Reilly, *Hoover and the Un-Americans: The FBI, HUAC, and the Red Menace* (Philadelphia, 1983), and Richard Criley, *The FBI v. the First Amendment* (Los Angeles, 1990), explore the FBI's covert relationship with the House Committee on Un-American Activities, including monitoring its critics. Herbert Mitgang, *Dangerous Dossiers: Exposing the Secret War Against America's Greatest Authors* (New York, 1988), and Natalie Robins, *Alien Ink: The FBI's War on Freedom of Expression* (New York, 1992), recount the FBI's monitoring of prominent writers, including Ernest Hemingway, Sinclair Lewis, Archibald MacLeish, Pearl Buck, and Robert Sherwood. Frank Donner, *Protectors of Privilege: Red Squads and Police Repression in Urban America* (Berkeley, Calif., 1990), describes the FBI's relationship with local police "Red Squads." Alexander Charns, *Cloak and Gavel: FBI Wiretaps, Bugs, Informers and the Supreme Court* (Urbana, Ill., 1992), offers insights into the FBI's monitoring of the Supreme Court. John D'Emilio, *Sexual Politics, Sexual Communities: The Making of a Homosexual Minority in the United States* (Chicago, 1983), is a brief survey of FBI surveillance of homosexuals. Cindy Jacquith and Diane Wang, *FBI vs. Women* (New York, 1977), reports on FBI surveillance of women's rights activists. Athan Theoharis, ed., *Beyond the Hiss Case: The FBI, Congress, and the Cold War* (Philadelphia, 1982), contains essays on FBI separate records procedures, break-ins, the Hiss case, and investigations of Vito Marcantonio, the American Labor party, the National Lawyers Guild, and the National Committee to Abolish HUAC.

Hoover has been the subject of a number of biographies. The best are those based on recently released FBI records, and include Athan Theoharis and John Stuart Cox, *The Boss: J. Edgar Hoover and the Great American Inquisition* (Philadelphia, 1988); Richard Gid Powers, *Secrecy and Power: The Life of J. Edgar Hoover* (New York, 1987); and Curt Gentry, *J. Edgar Hoover: The Man and the Secrets* (New York, 1991).

The post-Hoover FBI has been sketchily surveyed in Tony Poveda, *Lawlessness and Reform: The FBI in Transition* (Pacific Grove, Calif., 1990); Ralph Blumenthal, *Last Days of the Sicilians: At War with the Mafia* (New York, 1988); Ronald Kessler, *The FBI: Inside the World's Most Powerful Law Enforcement Agency* (New York, 1993); Ross Gelbspan, *Break-ins, Death Threats and the FBI* (Boston, 1991); and Gary Marx, *Undercover: Police Surveillance in America* (Berkeley, Calif., 1988).

The intensity of FBI surveillance of dissident political activities is further chronicled in recent biographies, whether of FBI informers—Ronald Reagan (Garry Wills, *Reagan's America*), Frank Capra (Joseph McBride, *Frank Capra*), and Walt Disney (Marc Eliot, *Walt Disney*)—or the targets of Hoover's surveillance interest—Martin Luther King (Taylor Branch, *Parting the Waters*), Eleanor

Roosevelt (Joseph Lash, *Love, Eleanor*), Margaret Sanger (Ellen Chesler, *Woman of Valor*), Owen Lattimore (Robert Newman, *Owen Lattimore and the "Loss" of China*), William Remington (Gary May, *Un-American Activities*), Malcolm X (Clayborn Carson, *Malcolm X*), Paul Robeson (Martin Duberman, *Paul Robeson*), Pete Seeger (David Dunaway, *How Can I Keep from Singing*), Bernarr Macfadden (Robert Ernst, *Weakness Is a Crime*), Emma Goldman (Candace Falk, *Love, Anarchy and Emma Goldman*), Tish Sommers (Patricia Huckle, *Tish Sommers, Activist, and the Founder of the Older Women's League*), Charles Chaplin (Charles Maland, *Chaplin and American Culture*), Clifford Durr (John Salmond, *The Conscience of a Lawyer*), and Ezra Pound (John Tytell, *Ezra Pound*).

Research for this book was based primarily on FBI records. Some of the documents quoted in the book are reprinted in Athan Theoharis, ed., *From the Secret Files of J. Edgar Hoover* (Chicago, 1991).

The Bohlen matter is from the Senator Joseph McCarthy and the Charles Bohlen folders in the Official and Confidential File of FBI Director J. Edgar Hoover (henceforth Hoover O&C). The Haldeman, Ehrlichman, and Chapin matter is from the Richard Nixon–Administration Organization Homosexuals in Government folder, Hoover O&C. The Sumner Welles matter is from the Sumner Welles folder, Hoover O&C. The homosexual allegations relating to Hoover are from the John Monroe and Name Withheld #75 and #113 folders, Hoover O&C, and The Director folder, Official and Confidential File of FBI Assistant Director Louis Nichols (henceforth Nichols O&C). The Leviero-Spivak matter is from the American Mercury folder, Nichols O&C. The Joseph Bryan matter is from the Joseph Bryan folder, Nichols O&C.

The Obscene File and White Slave Traffic Act matters are from SAC Letters File 66-04, Bureau Bulletins File 66-03, and Record Destruction File 66-3286. The summary memorandum matter is from Record Destruction File 66-3286. The Henry Cabot Lodge matter is from Henry Cabot Lodge folder, Hoover O&C. The William Anderson matter is from Congressman William Anderson folder, Hoover O&C. The monitoring of members of Congress is from Washington Field Division folder, Hoover O&C. The Senator Arthur Vandenberg matter is from Arthur Vandenberg folder, Hoover O&C. Kennedy's alleged affairs are from the Mrs. Paul Fejos, nee Inga Arvad, and the John F. Kennedy folders, Hoover O&C. The Eleanor Roosevelt matter is from the Joseph Lash folder, Hoover O&C, and the Dwight Eisenhower folder, Nichols O&C. The Dwight Eisenhower matter is from the Dwight Eisenhower folder, Nichols O&C. The Martin Luther King matter is from the Martin Luther King, Jr., folder, Hoover O&C, and Martin Luther King File 100-106670. References to the Sex Deviates program are included in the FBI's Responsibilities Program File 62-93875. The Adlai Stevenson matter is from the Adlai Stevenson, Jr., folders, Hoover O&C. The Nixon/Haldeman request re Washington press corps is from Personal File of FBI Associate Director Clyde Tolson. The Arthur Vandenberg, Jr., matter is from Arthur Vandenberg folder, Hoover O&C, and the Dwight Eisenhower folder, Nichols O&C. The White House mail room employees matter is from White House Employees–Homosexuals folder, Hoover O&C. The Joseph Alsop matter is from the Joseph Alsop folder, Hoover O&C.

The Courtney Ryley Cooper matter is from the FBI's Cooper File 94-3-4-20. Hoover's rules re agent conduct and appearance are from SAC Letters File 66-04 and Bureau Bulletins File 66-03. FBI surveillance of reporters, reports to the Roosevelt White House, and surveillance of Communists and fascists are from FBI, White House, and Francis Biddle records deposited at the Franklin D. Roosevelt presidential library, Hyde Park, New York. FBI relations with the House Committee on Un-American Activities (HUAC), the Senate Internal Security Subcommittee (SISS), Senator Joseph McCarthy, and with governors are from FBI HUAC File 61-7582; FBI SISS File 62-88217; FBI McCarthy Files 121-41668 and 94-37708; Senator Joseph McCarthy folder, Hoover O&C; Miscellaneous Memoranda folder, Nichols O&C; and FBI Responsibilities

Program File 62-93875. The wiretapping, break-in, and bugging policy and practice, Fred Black case, and Fortas matters are from "Black Bag" Jobs, Fred Black, Microphone Surveillance, Technical Surveillances, Wiretapping Presidential Authority, and Wiretapping Use of in FBI folders, Hoover O&C, and FBI Surreptitious Entries File 62-117166.

The Ernst *Reader's Digest* article matter is from Morris Ernst folder, Nichols O&C. The Karl Mundt matter is from Kenneth O'Reilly, *Hoover and the Un-Americans*, pp. 128, 338 n60.

INDEX

Adams, Sherman, 75, 112, 113
Administrative Index, 138n
Administrative pages, 68–69
Agnew, Spiro, 76
Alderisio, Phil, 158
Alderman, Willie, 158
Alsop, Joseph, 112–114, 168
Alstock, Francis, 91–92
American Mercury, 37
Anderson, Jack, 30–31, 43n
Anderson, William, 75–76,
    167–168
Angleton, James J., 46–47, 48
Apalachin, N.Y., 13, 139, 147, 153
Arnett, Peter, 136n
Arvad, Inga, 70n, 80–84, 96n, 168
Associated Press, 14
Attorney general, and FBI, 130,
    138n, 145–150, 151–153, 161–162

Balistrieri, Frank, 158
Barbara, Joseph, 139–140
Belmont, Alan, 147–148
Bernstein, Leonard, 136n
Berrigan, Daniel and William,
    75–76
Biddle, Francis, 130, 138n
Bishop, Thomas, 73n, 123
Black, Fred, 151–153, 169
Blossom, Sumner, 125
Bohlen, Charles, 24–29, 167
Bonanno, Joseph, 140
Bowles, Chester, 135

Bradlee, Ben, 97–98
Break-ins, 130, 133n, 142–145,
    150–151, 159, 169
Brewster, Ralph, 33
Bridges, Harry, 130
Browder, Earl, 131
Brownell, Herbert, 17, 112; and FBI
    bugging, 146–147, 152, 162
Brunette, Harry, 123
Bryan, Joseph III, 49–52, 167
Buchalter, Louis, 123
Budenz, Louis, 54
Bullitt, William, 32

Cagney, James, 125
Campbell, Judith, 84–85
Capell, Frank, 88
Central Intelligence Agency (CIA),
    46, 48, 49, 50, 52, 157
Chang, Suzy, 87
Chapin, Dwight, 30–31, 167
Chaplin, Charles, 136n
Chicago Tribune, 99, 130
Clark, Ramsey, 162
Clark, William, 45
Clinton, Bill, 15, 16
Cohn, Roy, 39, 40–41, 41n
COINTELPRO, 99, 133, 136, 159
Cold war, 127, 131–137, 138n, 162,
    164
Colson, Charles, 83
Communist party or Communists,
    68–69, 99, 128–134, 168

Congress: and FBI, 17, 18, 69–74, 75–78, 162, 163, 167–168; and homosexuals, 102–103
Conroy, E. E., 35
Conservatives: and anticommunism, 24–26, 135, 137, 162–164; and character assassination, 26–28, 78–79, 83–84, 87, 88, 90–92, 99, 106–109, 114; and "law and order," 138n; and states' rights, libertarian values, 60, 120
Cooper, Courtney Ryley, 124–125, 168
Coplon, Judith, 141, 141n, 145, 163
Counterintelligence Corps (CIC), 88–90, 90n
Croswell, Edgar, 139–140
Cummings, Homer, 122–123
Custodial Detention, 138n

Daughters of Bilitis, 24, 104n
Dean, John W. III, 161
DeLoach, Cartha, 30–31, 51, 72, 123, 152–153
Department of Justice: and legislation, 138n; and organized crime, 20, 148–150
Dewey, Thomas, 101n
Dillinger, John, 121, 123
Do Not File, 142, 145
Dole, Robert, 15
Donovan, William, 47
Douglas, Paul, 135
Dulles, Allen, 29, 112
Dulles, John Foster, 29, 92, 112
Durie, Malcolm, 86–87

Edwards, Don, 136
Ehrlichman, John, 12, 30–31, 167
Eisenhower, Dwight D., 23, 71n, 74, 168; and Bohlen nomination, 24–30; and Hoover, 92–96, 109–114, 146–148
Ernst, Morris, 163, 169
Esquire, 63n

Fair Play for Cuba Committee, 100
Federal Bureau of Investigation (FBI); and break-ins, 130, 136, 142–145, 150–151, 159, 169; and bugging, 130, 136, 151–153, 159, 162, 169; and COINTELPRO, 99, 133, 136, 159; and Congress, 132, 135–136; and Coplon case, 141, 141n, 145; and criminal investigations, 12–13, 16–18, 20, 139–154, 157–158; and "educational campaign," 131–132, 162; and homosexuals, 19, 23–33, 44–45, 74–75, 100–114, 166, 168; and informers, 139, 143, 154; and internal lawlessness, 19–20, 158–160; and labor unions, 129, 130, 131, 144; and Laboratory, 63; and media, 97, 113–114, 132–133; and National Academy, 127; and Obscene File, 19, 48–50, 62–65, 167; and other intelligence agencies, 46–52, 89n; and political surveillance, 59–60, 96–97, 130–131; and sexual activities, 16–17, 76–77, 80–115; and subversive activities, 127–139; and Top Hoodlum program, 140, 143–145, 147–150; and wiretapping, 130, 136, 138n, 140–142, 158, 160, 161–162, 169
Federal Communications Act of 1934, 138n, 140
Federal Employee Loyalty Program, 101, 103, 133–134, 137
Foreign Agent Registration Act, 131

Fortas, Abe, 152–153, 169
Fratianno, Jimmy, 53
"Frontline," 11, 14, 16
Fulbright, J. William, 45–46, 136

Gabrielson, Guy, 101–102
Galante, Carmine, 140
Gale, James, 149–150
Gandy, Helen, 73
Gay Activists Alliance, 104n
Gay Liberation Front, 104n
Genovese, Vito, 140
German American Bund, 128
Germany, 128, 130
Giancana, Sam, 84, 158
Goldwater, Barry, 80
Gary, Robert, 114

Haldeman, H. R., 30–31, 76, 108,
    167, 168
Hall, Leonard, 71n
Hemingway, Ernest, 136n
Henshaw, John, 93
Herter, Christian, 112, 114
Hill, Milt, 106–107
Hiss, Alger, 132, 133–135, 166
Hoey, Clyde, 102
Hoffa, James, 151
Holloman, F. C., 36
Hollywood, 121, 125
Homosexuals, 19, 23–33, 44–45,
    74–75, 100–114, 166, 168
Hood, Wayne, 71n
Hoover, J. Edgar, 59; and alleged
    blackmailing by Mob, 11, 15,
    17–18, 46–48, 52–53, 55; and
    alleged homosexuality, 11–17,
    20, 23, 33–52, 55, 167; and
    attorney general, 138n, 145–150,
    151–153, 161–162; and
    break-ins, 142–145, 150–151,
    159, 169; and bugging, 151–153,
    159, 162, 169; and Congress, 17,

18, 50–52, 53–54, 68–74, 75–78,
    135–136, 162, 163, 167–168; and
    criminal activities, 12–13,
    16–18, 20, 123, 139–154,
    157–158, 164; and "educational
    campaign," 131–132; and FBI
    agents, 125–126, 127, 136,
    142–143, 159, 168; and Fred
    Black case, 151–153; and
    homosexuals, 19, 23–33, 44–45,
    74–75, 100–114, 166, 168; and
    informers, 139, 143, 154; and
    "intelligence," 128n; and
    internal lawlessness, 19–20, 130,
    133, 133n, 158–160; and J. Edgar
    Hoover Foundation, 40; and
    media, 11, 14–16, 36–38, 80–84,
    96n, 97, 123–125, 130, 132–133,
    136, 162–163, 168; and Obscene
    File, 19, 48–50, 62–65, 167; and
    Official and Confidential File,
    73, 74, 77, 79, 82, 84, 107; and
    other intelligence agencies,
    46–52, 89n; and Personal and
    Confidential File, 73, 107; and
    preventive detention, 138n; and
    prominent persons, 70–71n, 157;
    and reform of Bureau, 60–61;
    and separate records procedures,
    68–71, 73, 81–82, 83, 93–94, 96,
    96n, 108–109n, 142, 157; and
    sexual activities, 12, 14, 16–17,
    19, 61, 65–69, 70n, 72, 80–100,
    164; and subversive activities,
    19, 53–54, 68–69, 96–99,
    127–139, 153, 164; and Top
    Hoodlum program, 140,
    143–145, 147–150; and White
    House, 17, 19, 23, 30–32, 79–80,
    82, 83–84, 107–114, 160–161,
    167, 168; and wiretapping,
    140–142, 158, 160, 161–162, 169

House Committee on
  Un-American Activities
  (HUAC), 53, 54, 132, 168
Hull, Cordell, 33
Humphreys, Robert, 71n
Huston, Tom Charles, 160
Hyde, Herbert, 93–94

Internal Security (McCarran) Act
  of 1950, 138n
Irvine v. California, 146

Jackson, Robert, 161
Jenkins, Walter, 80, 111n
Jenner, William, 50, 52
Johnson, Lyndon B., 18, 46, 111n,
  161; and Hoover, 79–80, 152,
  152–153n
Johnston, Stanley, 130
Jones, Milton, 74

Karpis, Alvin, 123
Kater, Florence, 85–86
Katzenbach, Nicholas deB., 97,
  153n; and FBI bugging, 148–150,
  148–149n; and Hoover, 162
Kelley, Clarence, 157
Kelly, George, 123
Kennedy, Edward, 84
Kennedy, John F., 70n, 80–88, 169
Kennedy, Robert, 13, 17, 85, 87,
  88, 152
King, Martin Luther, Jr., 96–98,
  135, 166, 168
Kleindienst, Richard, 43n

Lansky, Meyer, 158
Lash, Joseph, 89–92
Lawrence, David, 132
Le Ore, 85
Leno, Jay, 14–15
Leviero, Anthony, 37–38, 167
Lewis, Fulton, Jr., 93, 132

Lincoln, Evelyn, 84–85
Lindbergh, Charles, 121
Lisagor, Peter, 136n
Lodge, Henry Cabot, 71n, 74–75,
  167
Long, Edward, 152
Lord, Mary, 90–91
Los Angeles Times, 37
Lowenthal, Max, 163
Lucchesi, Thomas, 140

Macdonald, Dwight, 136n
Magaddino, Stefano, 140
Mailer, Norman, 136
Manchester Union Leader, 87
Manly, Chesly, 130
Mann Act. *See* White Slave Traffic
  Act.
Marcello, Carlos, 158
Marshall, George, 89
Marshall, Thurgood, 151
Mass Media program, 132, 159
Mattachine Society, 24, 104n
Matusow, Harvey, 54
McCarthy, Joseph, 94–96, 100–102,
  132, 168; and Hoover, 26–29
McElroy, Neil, 114
McFarlin, M. W., 36
McGovern, George, 73–74n, 136
McGrath, J. Howard, 17; and FBI
  bugging, 145–146; and FBI
  wiretapping, 141n
McPhee, Henry, 111n
Microphone surveillance (or
  bugging), 130, 143, 151–153,
  159, 162, 169
Military Intelligence Division
  (MID), 47
Mitchell, John, 17, 31, 76, 138n
Monroe, John, 33–34, 167
Monroe, Marilyn, 88
Morse, Wayne, 136

Mundt, Karl, 163–164, 169
Murphy, George, 91–92

National Archives, and FBI files, 66–67, 67n, 104
Nelson, Jack, 37, 71
New Deal, 61
New Left, 133
New York Daily News, 66, 130
New York Post, 92
New Yorker, 15
Nichols, Louis, 34, 37, 38, 40, 51–52, 53, 67n, 75, 78, 79, 81, 83, 90n, 91–92, 93–95, 106–107, 109–110, 123, 163
Nixon, Richard, 75–76, 157; and crime, 17–18, 138n; and Hoover, 30–31, 83–84, 107–109, 111n, 160–161, 167, 168; and obscenity, 64; and wiretapping, 160
Norris, George, 136
Novel, Gordon, 46–47, 48
Novotny, Marie, 87
Noyes, Newbold, 132

Obscene File, 19, 48–50, 62–65, 167
Office of Naval Intelligence (ONI), 47
Office of Strategic Services (OSS), 46–49, 52
Omnibus Crime Control and Safe Streets Act, 158
One, 24
Oursler, Fulton, 163–164, 169
Owen, David, 106

Palmer, Paul, 38
Papich, Sam, 52
Patterson, Eleanor, 130
Patterson, J. M., 66, 130
Pearson, Drew, 30–31, 34n

Pepper, Claude, 136
Persons, Wilton, 114
Pollack, Seymour, 53, 55
Pornography. *See* Obscene File.
Profaci, Joseph, 140
Prohibition, 61, 121
Purdom, Alicia, 85, 87

Racketeering Influence Corrupt Organization Act (RICO), 137–138, 138n, 158
Reader's Digest, 38, 163, 169
Reid, Ogden, 93
Remington, William, 133–135, 167
Resnick, Irving, 53
Responsibilities Program, 132, 168
Reuss, Henry, 72n
Reuters, 14
Reuther, Walter, 135
Roberts, Wesley, 71n
Robertson, Betsy, 78
Rogers, William, 112, 114, 148, 152
Rometsch, Ellen, 87
Roosevelt, Eleanor, 89–92, 135, 167, 168
Roosevelt, Franklin D., 75, 82; and crime, 17–18, 121–123, 126; and Hoover, 32–33, 129–131, 168; and New Deal, 120; and wiretapping, 141, 161
Roosevelt, James, 136
Roselli, John, 84, 158
Rosenberg, Julius and Ethel, 133–135
Rosenstiel, Lewis, 40–43
Rosenstiel, Susan, 39–43, 44, 55
Ruffin, Marshall deG., 43–45, 43n

Scalisi, John, 140
Schlesinger, Arthur M., Jr., 135
Security Index, 138n
Seeger, Pete, 136n

Senate Internal Security Subcommittee (SISS), 50, 52, 53, 132, 168
Sessions, William, 15, 157
Sex Deviates program, 23–24, 103–106, 168
Smith Act, 53–54, 134, 137
Sokolsky, George, 132
Sourwine, Jay, 52
Soviet Union, 128, 130
Spivak, Lawrence, 37–38, 167
Startzell, James, 75–76
Stevenson, Adlai, 71n, 105–107, 135, 168
Stone, Harlan Fiske, 59, 61
Sullivan, William, 71–72, 71n, 98, 158–159n, 160
Summary (or final) memorandum procedure, 69–71, 73, 74, 167
Summers, Anthony, 11–17, 20, 39, 43, 46, 53, 55
Summersby, Kay, 94–96
Supreme Court, 18, 64, 151–152
Surine, Don, 94–96
Suydam, Henry, 122

Tolson, Clyde, 12, 37, 38
Top Hoodlum program, 140, 143–145, 147–150
Trafficante, Santos, 140
Trohan, Walter, 132
Truman, Harry S, 47, 91; and Hoover, 132; and homosexuals in government, 100–102; and wiretapping, 141

USA Today, 14, 16

Vandenberg, Arthur, 78–79, 96, 168
Vandenberg, Arthur, Jr., 79, 109–111, 111n, 168
Vanity Fair, 11, 16
Vitale, John, 93, 96

Waldrop, Frank, 78–79, 90–91
Wallace, George, 138n
Wallace, Henry, 135
Washington Times-Herald, 78, 81, 82, 90–91, 130
Watergate, 161
Watkins, Arthur, 90–91
Webster, William, 157
Weitz, John, 46, 52
Welch, Neil, 159
Welles, Sumner, 32–33, 167
Wheeler, Burton, 32
Wherry, Kenneth, 101n
White House, and Hoover, 17, 18, 19, 23, 30–32, 79–80, 160–161
White Slave Traffic (or Mann) Act, 65–68, 144, 167
Whitehead, Don, 132
Wilson, Lyle, 132
Winchell, Walter, 132
Wiretapping, 130, 133n, 138n, 140–142, 158, 161–162, 169
Woltman, Frederick, 132
World War II, 127–131

Yalta Conference, 25, 26
Yarger, Orval, 106–107

A NOTE ON THE AUTHOR

For more than a decade Athan Theoharis has been the most diligent historian and critic of the Federal Bureau of Investigation, based upon his intensive research in the Bureau's files under the Freedom of Information Act. His other books include *The Boss: J. Edgar Hoover and the Great American Inquisition; From the Secret Files of J. Edgar Hoover; Beyond the Hiss Case; Spying on Americans; The Specter; Seeds of Repression; The Yalta Myths;* and *Anatomy of Anti-Communism.* Mr. Theoharis studied history at the University of Chicago, taught at Texas A&M University, Wayne State University, and the City University of New York, and is now professor of history at Marquette University. He is married and the father of three children, and lives in Milwaukee.